THE
COUNTRY
DIARY
COOKERY
NOTES

Red Campion
(Lychnis diurna)
Wild Hyacinth
(agraphis nutans)
Wild Beaked Parsley
(anthriscus sylvestris)

THE COUNTRY DIARY

COOKERY NOTES

Sloe or Blackthorn
(Prunus communis)

Spray of budding
Crab-apple

Edith Holden/Alison Harding

Bloomsbury Books
London

First published in Great Britain 1984 by
Webb & Bower (Publishers) Limited
9 Colleton Crescent, Exeter, Devon EX2 4BY

Copyright © Richard Webb Limited 1984
Text Copyright © Alison Harding 1984

Designed by Peter Wrigley

The publishers would like to thank Rowena Stott, Edith Holden's
great-niece and the owner of the original work, who has made the
publication of this book possible.

First impression September 1984
Second impression April 1987
Third impression February 1988

This edition published 1993 by
Bloomsbury Books, an imprint of
The Godfrey Cave Group,
42 Bloomsbury Street, London WC1B 3QJ,
under licence from Webb & Bower Ltd 1993.

ISBN 1-85471-133-4

Printed and bound by BPCC Paulton Books Ltd.

CONTENTS

Hazel Nuts (Corylus avellana)

INTRODUCTION

There are few more pleasurable or nostalgic pastimes than leafing through the hand-written notebooks of cooks and housekeepers who have carefully recorded the hints and recipes used in their day-to-day lives. Like the illustrated nature diary compiled by Edith Holden, such collections indicate a conscientious preoccupation with detail and a practical concern with their subject — an approach which the writers must have applied to even the most repetitive of their routine housekeeping tasks. Edwardian cooks, like their predecessors, took pride and pleasure in their work. And though it is now more fashionable to take short cuts in the preparation of meals, to replace old methods and ingredients with the latest gadgets or convenience foods, there is still much to be learned and enjoyed from trying out some of those old-fashioned instructions.

Part of this 'Edwardian' collection consists of recipes for familiar, classic dishes which were just as popular almost a hundred years ago as they are today; among them appear other recipes which have perhaps lain forgotten for a generation or two, but which are well worth trying again. It has been necessary for the sake of clarity to update such technicalities as quantities and temperatures — the 'handfuls' or 'small teacupfuls' of the original versions might otherwise lead to disaster. With some recipes, particularly those for soups or jams and other preserves, the originals have had to be scaled down to suit our smaller households or less prolific gardens. But I have tried to retain something of the style and 'atmosphere' of the manuscripts, newspaper scraps or well-thumbed leaflets from which the material for this book has been gleaned.

In trying to achieve the somewhat daunting aim of putting together a collection that might have been familiar to Edith Holden and her contemporaries, I have chosen recipes that could have been used in any respectable household of the day — a period when families tended to be large, and the products of garden and countryside were utilized in many well-tried, ingenious ways. Some of these were part of the housekeeping lore handed down over the centuries; others had developed during the more recent industrial revolution, which increased the ideas, materials, and equipment available to many housewives and cooks. While it has proved possible only to indicate the variety and detail of the original sources, I hope that present-day cooks will find interest in this notebook, as well as pleasure in knowing that their art, like that of their predecessors earlier this century, is part of a tradition which remains both lively and productive.

1 *SOUPS*

SOUPS

Visited a small wood on the canal bank, to get violet leaves. On moving away some of the dead leaves lying beneath the trees, I discovered a Wild Arum plant.

Common Garlic
(allium ursinum)

STOCK

At one time cooks relied upon having a stock-pot always at the ready when they came to make soup. Though we do not need to do this now, having good commercial stock-cubes or powders available, it is useful to be able to make a simple stock when occasion demands — and of course it can make all the difference to the flavour of home-made soups, sauces and stews.

Bones and other unwanted parts of joints, poultry, game and fish can be used in conjunction with vegetables and herbs. Chicken or lamb make a white stock, beef or game a strong brown stock; ham or bacon should be used with care as it may be very salty and need preliminary boiling or soaking, but it makes a good base for some vegetable soups. Cooked bones and meat will make a darker, stronger-tasting stock than uncooked. All stocks should be carefully skimmed, and those containing fatty material should be cooled, skimmed, and boiled again before use. The following basic recipes can be varied according to the ingredients available.

MEAT STOCK

2 lb/1 kg/2 lb shin of beef or other meat, bones, etc.
1 large carrot
1 onion
1/2 small turnip
2 sticks celery
1/2 tsp mixed dried herbs or sprigs of fresh thyme, basil, parsley
1 bay leaf
6 peppercorns
1-2 tsp salt

Wipe meat or crack bones, removing any pieces of fat; place the meat in a large pan with the cleaned vegetables and the herbs. Cover well with water, bring to the boil, then skim. Replace on heat and simmer steadily for 3 hours, skimming occasionally if necessary. Strain the stock, and if it is fatty allow it to cool, then remove any fat from the surface before use.

VEGETABLE STOCK

This is very useful for making light soups or sauces, or it can be used with eggs and fish, as well as for vegetable dishes.

1 large carrot
1 large onion
1 leek (green and white parts)
1 small turnip
1 stick celery
1 tsp salt
6 peppercorns
1/4 tsp mixed dried herbs or sprigs of thyme and parsley
1 bay leaf
3 pt/ 1 3/4 l/ 8 cups water

SOUPS

Sharp frost and thick fog in the early morning. The fog cleared off about 9.30. A.m. and the sun shone brightly. Went for a country walk.

Common Garlic
(allium ursinum)

Clean the vegetables, peel thinly if necessary but for preference simply scrub them; slice them all roughly, then put them in a pan with water, herbs and seasonings. Bring to the boil, skim, simmer briskly for about 1 hour, then strain before using. This gives a white stock; if brown vegetable stock is needed, place about 2 oz/ 50 g/ ½ stick of butter in the pan, and cook the vegetables gently in this with the lid off, until they brown. Then add water and cook as above.

FISH STOCK

2 lb/1 kg/2 lb fish trimmings (head, skin, bones)
1 onion, chopped
1 carrot, chopped
2 sticks celery, chopped

4 peppercorns
1 bay leaf
1 sprig fennel or parsley
1 tsp salt

Put all the ingredients into a large pan, cover with water and bring to the boil. Simmer for 1 hour, then strain and use, adding a small glass of white wine if you wish.

Substantial old-fashioned soups often required more meat than we would use today. They were usually served as two courses, meat and vegetables following the broth in which they were cooked; now we would probably serve them as a stew, accompanied by potatoes or rice.

THICK OXTAIL SOUP

A classic English soup, somewhat neglected in recent years, this makes an excellent main course. A fresh oxtail is best, but some butchers keep a supply of frozen tails; herbs, too, should be fresh if possible.

1 oxtail
6 oz/150 g/³/4 cup chopped lean ham or bacon
2 oz/50 g/2 tbsp butter or dripping
2 large onions, 2 carrots, 1 small turnip, 1 parsnip
4 pt/2 l/10 cups water or meat stock
2 oz/50 g/¹/2 cup flour

2 sticks celery, chopped
1 tsp dried mixed herbs or a sprig each of thyme, basil and marjoram, and a bay leaf, tied together
1 tsp chopped parsley
salt and ground black pepper to taste

Wipe and joint the oxtail, removing any large pieces of fat. Melt the butter in a large pan, add the pieces of tail, chopped bacon and

SOUPS

Every twig on every tree and bush was outlined in silver tracery against the sky; some of the dead grasses and seed-vessels growing by the road-side were specially beautiful.

Common Garlic
(Allium ursinum)

sliced onions; cook until well browned, then sprinkle over the flour, and continue to cook until this too is browned. Boil the stock separately, then add to the meat and onions a little at a time, stirring to mix it smoothly with the flour. Bring to the boil, add the herbs and salt, then the remaining vegetables, chopped quite small. Simmer the soup until the meat is tender (about 2 hours) then add the celery and parsley with the ground pepper. If preferred, the larger pieces of tail may be served separately with mashed or boiled potatoes, and green vegetables — sprouts or spinach are good with this. A little freshly ground nutmeg, or for special occasions, a glass of port, may be added to the soup before serving for extra flavour.

PHEASANT SOUP

Any game bird of small size or doubtful age can be used for this. One large or two small birds make a good dish, served whole, with creamed potatoes and sprouts or broccoli, after the broth.

1 pheasant
2 oz/50 g/¹/₂ cup flour
1 oz/25 g/2 tbsp butter or dripping
4 oz/125 g/¹/₂ cup chopped lean ham or bacon
2 onions
¹/₂ head of celery

2 pt/1 l/5 cups water or vegetable stock
salt and ground black pepper to taste
2 oz/50 g/1 cup soft breadcrumbs
yolks of 2 hard-boiled eggs
1 small glass sherry or madeira

Joint the bird (unless using as a main course), flour it well and place it in a large pan with the butter, already melted but not brown. Cook gently till the bird is browned, then remove to a warm dish. Add the ham, sliced onions and roughly chopped celery to the pan, and cook in the remaining butter till soft; cover with salted water, bring to the boil and replace the bird, then simmer in the broth for about 2 hours until tender. For a light soup, remove the bird and vegetables carefully, strain the broth, then add the breadcrumbs, mashed egg yolks, and, unless needed for a main course, the finely chopped breast of the bird. Season with pepper and add the sherry before serving. If a thicker soup is preferred, retain the bacon and vegetables with the above additions and further meat from the bird.

SOUPS

I saw great flocks of Rooks and Starlings, down on the fields, and a pair of beautiful Bullfinches in a Hawthorn bush.

Common Garlic
(allium ursinum)

JENNY LIND'S SOUP

Soups made from stock and eggs are simple and sustaining.

2 oz/50 g/¹/₃ cup of sago or tapioca
2 pt/1¹/₄ l/5 cups beef or veal stock
2 egg yolks
¹/₄ pt/150 ml/²/₃ cup cream or milk
1 pt/600 ml/2¹/₂ cups water
salt and pepper to taste

Simmer the sago and water together over a low heat until the sago is thick and soft. Mix in gradually the cream and the beaten egg yolks, then the heated stock, stirring gently so that the eggs do not curdle. Season with salt, and white pepper or a little freshly ground nutmeg.

CREAM OF SALMON SOUP

A simple, useful recipe for using left-over salmon.

8 oz/225 g/¹/₂ lb cooked salmon,
    without bones
2 pt/1¹/₄ l/5 cups milk or half milk,
    half fish stock
¹/₂ small onion
1 oz/25 g/2 tbsp butter
1 oz/25 g/¹/₄ cup flour
1 tsp salt
1 bay leaf

Heat the milk with the onion and bay leaf; remove from heat. Melt the butter in a second pan, add the flour and stir well. Take the onion and bay leaf from the milk, then add this to the flour and butter stirring all the time to keep the mixture smooth. Add the flaked salmon and the salt, and cook very gently for about 20 minutes over a low heat, stirring frequently. Add the lemon juice and parsley then serve at once.

CREAM OF CRAB OR LOBSTER SOUP

These soups may be made in the same way as salmon soup, using the flaked flesh of cooked lobster or crab. If less flesh is available, the chopped whites and mashed yolks of two hard-boiled eggs can be added just before serving, but omit the lemon juice.

EEL SOUP

A simple tasty soup, for which either small eels or pieces of conger eel may be used.

1 lb/500 g/1 lb eel
1¹/₂ pt/1 l/4 cups fish stock
2 egg yolks

The green leaves are out on the Woodbine too making little spots of green among the under--growth.

Common Garlic
(Allium ursinum)

Remove the skin from the eel and cut it into small pieces; salt them lightly and leave for about 1 hour, then rinse off the salt. Place the eel in the stock in a large pan, bring to the boil and simmer for 30 minutes or until tender. Blend the egg yolks with a little of the soup in a bowl, then add them to the pan, stir well, and do not allow to boil. Add further seasoning to taste if needed.

POTATO CREAM SOUP

Almost any white vegetable can be combined with potatoes to make a delicious and versatile soup, which can be garnished with parsley, chives, grated cheese or nutmeg, or just a sprinkle of black or cayenne pepper. Older potatoes are best for the following recipe but if using new ones, they will not need to be sieved or mashed.

1 lb/500 g/1 lb potatoes
1 small onion
2 sticks celery or white part of
  1 large leek
1 oz/25 g/2 tbsp butter
1/4 pt/150 ml/2/3 cup cream or
  1/2 pt/300 ml/1 1/4 cups milk

1 1/2 pt/900 ml/3 3/4 cups water or
  light stock or milk and water
1/2 tsp salt
1 tbsp chopped parsley or chives
ground black pepper to taste

Peel or scrape the potatoes, slice thinly and rinse in cold water before using. Melt the butter in a large pan, add all the vegetables thinly sliced and stew them gently for 10 minutes, shaking the pan occasionally to avoid sticking. Add the liquid and salt, bring to the boil, stir well and simmer for about 1 hour or until the vegetables are soft. Then sieve or mash the vegetables, or leave in slices if preferred, and add the cream or milk. Reheat, season with pepper and salt to taste and garnish with parsley or chives before serving. An extra knob of butter can also be added if you wish.

TOMATO SOUP

1 lb/500 g/1 lb tomatoes
2 pt/1 1/4 l/5 cups water or stock
1 oz/25 g/1/4 cup flour
1 oz/25 g/2 tbsp butter
1 small onion
1 small carrot
1 stick celery

1/2 tsp salt
1/4 tsp ground cloves or nutmeg
1/4 pt/150 ml/2/3 cup cream or milk
1/2 tsp lemon juice
1 tsp sugar
ground black pepper to taste

Melt the butter in a large pan; add the thinly sliced onion, carrot and celery. Cook gently for a few minutes until soft, then add the thinly sliced tomatoes, and cook them for a further 5 minutes; shake the

SOUPS

Dull day with slight drizzle of rain in the morning but bright and mild in the afternoon.

Common Garlic
(Allium ursinum)

flour over the tomatoes and stir until mixed, then pour in the stock, seasoned with the salt and cloves. Bring to the boil, stirring to prevent the vegetables from sticking, and simmer for about 1 hour. The soup may then be put through a coarse sieve if you prefer, but the flavour is better if you don't do this. Add the sugar and lemon juice, stir well, and reheat if necessary before adding the cream, but do not allow the soup to boil. Add ground black pepper to taste; if you wish, a small slice of fresh bread or some soft breadcrumbs may be placed in each soup bowl before serving.

Vegetable soup need not be boring or predictable. Many good old-fashioned recipes use ingredients not always thought of nowadays for use in soup; here are some examples.

MARROW SOUP

Pieces of a large vegetable marrow may be used, but pumpkin or courgettes (zucchini) are also suitable.

1 lb/500 g/1 lb marrow pieces, without skin or seeds, or whole courgettes (zucchini)
1 large onion
1/2 lb/250 g/1 cup sliced tomatoes
2 oz/50 g/1/4 cup lean ham or bacon, chopped
1 1/2 pt/900 ml/3 3/4 cups water or stock

1/2 tsp salt
1 bay leaf, and a sprig of thyme
2 oz/50 g/1/2 stick butter
1 tbsp cream
ground black pepper or nutmeg to taste

Cook the bacon, chopped onion and sliced tomatoes in the melted butter in a large pan until soft and slightly brown. Add the marrow, chopped into small pieces, the herbs and salt, then the hot stock. Simmer until the vegetables are soft; sieve or mash the vegetables, reheat the soup, then add pepper or nutmeg to taste, a little more salt if needed, and finally the cream. Stir gently and do not boil, then serve with crisp bread rolls. A tablespoon of long grained rice or coarse oatmeal, put in after the vegetables are mashed, makes a good addition, the soup then needs cooking for about 20 minutes longer.

SPRING HERBS SOUP

The essentials for this soup are fresh green spring leaves, preferably a variety although it can be made using spinach or lettuce only. Spinach can be used where sorrel or other wild leaves are not available. Cabbage type lettuces are most suitable.

1 large or 2 small lettuces	*1 oz/25 g/2 tbsp butter*
a handful each of dandelion, sorrel and chervil leaves	*1 oz/25 g/¹/₄ cup flour*
	¹/₂ tsp salt
2 shallots or 2 spring onions (scallions)	*white pepper to taste*
	1 tsp white sugar
1 pt/600 ml/2¹/₂ cups white stock	*2 egg yolks*
¹/₂ pt/300 ml/1¹/₄ cups milk	*1 tbsp chopped parsley or chives*

Wash all the leaves carefully in several changes of well salted water; drain well and shred finely. Melt the butter in a large pan, cook the finely chopped shallots or spring onions for a few minutes then add all the leaves and the seasonings. Shake the pan several times to distribute the butter, then sprinkle in the flour and add the hot stock a little at a time, stirring to blend well. Simmer the soup gently for about 15 minutes, stirring several times. Heat the milk separately, add the sugar to it, and add this to the soup. Reheat the soup without boiling, then mix a little with the egg yolks in the bowl from which the soup is to be served. Pour in the rest of the soup very gradually and serve at once, garnished with the parsley or chives, or the green part of the spring onions.

CHESTNUT SOUP

1 lb/500 g/1 lb chestnuts	*1 oz/25 g/¹/₄ cup cornflour (cornstarch)*
1 pt/600 ml/2¹/₂ cups chicken stock	
1 pt/600 ml/2¹/₂ cups milk	*salt and cayenne pepper to taste*

Prepare the chestnuts by slitting the skins with a knife; then either put them in a hot oven for 15 minutes, and remove the skins; or boil them for 5 minutes in a pan of water and skin them one at a time. Heat the stock and peeled chestnuts, boil, then simmer for about 30 minutes until the chestnuts are soft enough to be either pressed through a coarse sieve, or mashed in the stock — a potato masher is good for this job. In a separate pan, melt the butter, add the cornflour and mix well, then gradually add the warmed milk. Pour this mixture into the chestnut purée, mix all together till smooth, reheat and season with salt and cayenne pepper to taste. For a richer flavour add a small piece of butter and a tablespoonful of cream before serving.

2 *FISH*

DEVILLED WHITEBAIT	23	JUGGED KIPPERS	27
BROWNED CRAB	23	BOILED SALMON	27
POTTED HERRINGS	25	FISH AND TOMATO PIE	28
POTTED SHRIMPS	25	KEDGEREE	28
TROUT WITH OATMEAL	25		

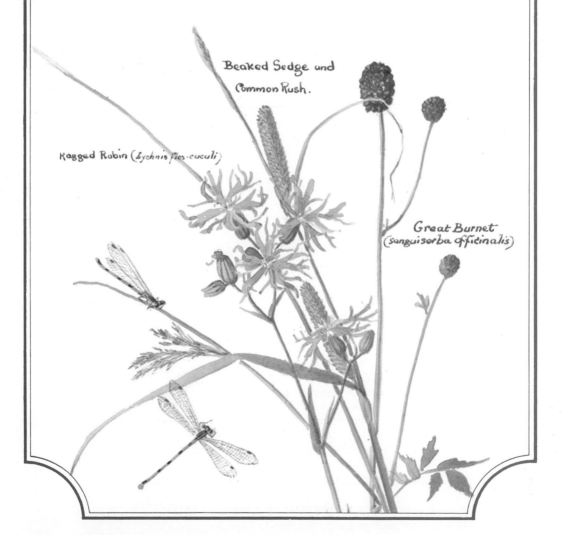

Beaked Sedge and Common Rush.

Ragged Robin (*Lychnis flos-cuculi*)

Great Burnet (*sanguisorba officinalis*)

FISH

I swept a space free on the lawn and strewed it with bread and rice. Crowds of birds came. I counted eight Tits at one time on the cocoa-nut and the tripod of sticks supporting it.

Bilberry or Whortleberry (*Vacoinium myrtilis*)
Painted Lady Butterfly (*Vanessa atalanta*)

There are many good old recipes for cooking fish, so that even the most common varieties need not be dull to eat. Most of these traditional dishes are fairly simple but the fish should always be as fresh as possible or, if frozen, thoroughly thawed before use.

DEVILLED WHITEBAIT

These small tasty fish have long been a London speciality. They are easily damaged, so should be handled carefully and cooked very quickly.

1 lb/¹/₂ kg/1 lb fresh whitebait
4 oz/125 g/1 cup flour
¹/₄ tsp salt

¹/₂ tsp ground black pepper
cayenne pepper to taste
lard or oil

Rinse the fish in plenty of cold water, pat them dry. Mix the salt with the flour, and shake half the flour over a clean cloth or paper. Place the fish on this, shake the remaining flour over and shake the cloth gently so that they are well coated. Fry them a few at a time in deep fat in a pan with a wire basket so that they can easily be removed. The fat should be very hot so they will need cooking for only a minute or two. They may be drained and served at once with sliced lemon and brown bread, or devilled as follows:

When the fish are cooked, lift and shake the pan and sprinkle in a little salt and some black pepper, then put the basket back into the fat for a few moments. Take it out again, drain, and serve the fish sprinkled with a little cayenne pepper if you wish them to be 'red devils'.

BROWNED CRAB

1 medium-sized crab
1 small onion
1 oz/25 g/¹/₄ cup chopped
  mushroom

1 oz/25 g/¹/₄ cup dried breadcrumbs
1 tbsp chopped parsley
¹/₂ oz/15 g/1 tbsp butter
salt and pepper to taste

Remove the crab from its shell and finely chop or mince the good flesh; wash, dry and lightly butter the shell. Melt a little more butter in a small pan, put in the finely chopped or minced onion, mushrooms and crab flesh, and season with salt and pepper. Stir until well heated, then put the mixture into the crab shell, cover with breadcrumbs and small pieces of butter, and brown in a hot oven or under a grill. Served hot in the shell, and garnished with a slice of lemon, this makes a delicious first course.

Heard the lark singing for the first time this year.
Cycled to Packwood through Solihull and Bentley-heath. I passed a rookery on the way, the Rooks were all very busy building up their old nests, and a great deal of chatter they made over it.

Bilberry or Whortleberry (Vacoinium myrtilis)
Painted Lady Butterfly (Vanessa atalanta)

POTTED HERRINGS

4 herrings
1/4 pt/150 ml/2/3 cup malt vinegar
1/4 pt/150 ml/2/3 cup water
1 small onion or 4 shallots

1/4 tsp salt
8 peppercorns
2 cloves
1 bay leaf

Wash, clean and fillet the herrings. Dry them and roll them up from tail to head, with the skins outside. Slice the onion finely then add it to the other ingredients, all mixed together. Put the herrings in an ovenproof dish, pour the vinegar mixture over and cook in a slow oven (300°F/150°C/Mark 2) for about 1 hour. Though usually served cold with a green salad, this dish is delicious hot, with crisp bread or baked jacket potatoes. Mackerel are also good cooked and served in this way, especially with one or two sliced tomatoes put in with the fish.

POTTED SHRIMPS

1/2 pt/300 ml/1 1/4 cups shrimps,
  cooked and shelled
3 oz/75 g/3/4 stick butter
1 tsp anchovy essence or lemon
  juice

1/4 tsp ground nutmeg
salt and ground black pepper

Melt 2 oz/50 g/1/2 stick butter in a saucepan, and heat the shrimps and butter together gently. When hot, remove them and pound the mixture. Season, add the essence or lemon juice, and sieve and pot.

TROUT WITH OATMEAL

Herring and mackerel are often cooked in this traditional Scottish way, which is very good with small, freshly caught trout.

4 trout
4 oz/125 g/1 cup medium or coarse
  oatmeal

1/4 tsp salt
pepper to taste
butter or dripping

Wash, clean and dry the fish, which may be filleted if preferred but are tastier left whole. Roll them well in the oatmeal. Melt enough butter in a heavy pan to well cover the base; when this is hot but not burning, place the trout in it. Cook the fish quickly, adding more fat if necessary when turning them over. When they are brown on both sides, remove them and drain them on kitchen paper, then serve very hot.

I saw a little Robin gathering materials for its nest, at one place on the bank and further on, a Thrush with a beakful of long straws:

Bilberry or Whortleberry *(Vacoinium myrtilis)*
Painted Lady Butterfly *(Vanessa atalanta)*

JUGGED KIPPERS

Nowadays kippers are usually grilled, but if you prefer them juicy, or wish to use them cold in another dish, such as kedgeree, the old method of using boiling water is better. A large saucepan can be used instead of the traditional jug, but fresh kippers are better than frozen.

pair fresh kippers
sufficient water to cover
mustard or sliced lemon

Heat the water to boiling point in the pan, remove from the heat and put in the kippers, heads down. Leave them to soak for at least 5 minutes, with the lid on the pan, then remove and serve on hot plates with mustard sauce (see page 59) or garnished with sliced lemon. A small piece of butter can be put on each kipper if you wish.

BOILED SALMON

Either a small whole fish or a large middle cut may be cooked this way, but the salmon should be as young and fresh as possible for the best flavour. When cooked, it can either be served cold in the classic way, with mayonnaise, or is very good hot, with a sauce made from the cooking liquor. The same method can be used for sea-trout.

1 salmon, or large cut, about
  3 lb/1.5 kg/3 lb
1 small carrot
1 small onion or 4 shallots
sprigs of parsley, fennel, thyme
1 bay leaf

1 tsp salt
1 tsp lemon juice or 1 large slice
  lemon
1 glass white wine
water to cover the fish

Clean and wash the fish, keeping on the head and tail if you have a pan large enough and wish to serve the salmon whole. It will be easier to handle and cook if you have a small metal rack that will nearly fit the bottom of the pan, which should be as wide as possible. Put the herbs and vegetables into the pan, half fill it with water, add the salt, and bring to the boil, then skim. Put in the salmon carefully, and add a little more hot water if needed to cover it. Add the lemon juice and wine, bring to the boil again and skim if necessary, then leave to simmer until the fish is tender, about 40 minutes. Allow the liquor to cool sufficiently for the fish to be removed; then either keep the salmon hot while making the sauce, or leave it to get cold before decorating it with parsley and sliced cucumber.

FISH AND TOMATO PIE

Any left-over cooked white fish is suitable for this recipe; tinned tomatoes may be used, but should be drained.

1/2 lb/225 g/1 1/2 cups fish
1/2 lb/225 g/4 cups soft breadcrumbs
1/2 lb/225 g/1 cup sliced tomatoes
2 beaten eggs
1/4 tsp cayenne or ground black
  pepper

1/4 tsp salt
1 oz/25 g/2 tbsp butter
2 oz/50 g/1/2 cup grated cheese
  (Cheddar type)

Flake the fish with a fork, discard any skin or bone. Butter a baking-dish and place in it the fish mixed with the breadcrumbs and seasonings; if tinned tomatoes are used mix these in with the fish. Put the fish mixture in the dish, cover with a layer of sliced tomatoes, and sprinkle the cheese over. Bake in a moderate oven (350°F/180°C/Mark 4) for about 30 minutes.

KEDGEREE

This very easy dish was once popular for breakfast but is now more useful for a quickly prepared lunch or supper. Either white or smoked fish (such as haddock or kippers) is suitable, and though usually served hot, it is just as tasty cold with a salad.

1 cup cold cooked flaked fish
1 cup cold cooked rice
2 eggs, hard-boiled or beaten
2 oz/50 g/1/2 stick butter

1 tsp chopped parsley
salt and ground black pepper to
  taste
1/4 tsp mustard powder (optional)

Melt the butter in a heavy pan, add the rice, stir well, and then add the fish, previously flaked with a fork. Add both eggs, well beaten, or one hard-boiled egg, chopped small. Stir, heat very well for about 5 minutes, then season and serve on a very hot dish, or allow to cool and serve with a green or tomato salad. Use the second hard-boiled egg to garnish the kedgeree.

3 MEAT, POULTRY AND GAME

Orange-tip Butterfly
(Euchloe Cardimines)

Oxe-eye Daisy
(Chrysanthemum leucanthamum)

Meadow Fox-Tail Grass
(Alopecurus pratensis)

Purple Clover
(Trifolium pratense)

MEAT, POULTRY AND GAME

Everywhere the branches of the Willow bushes were tipped with downy white balls and the Alder-catkins were shewing very red.

Juniper berries
(Juniperus
communis)

ROAST BEEF AND YORKSHIRE PUDDING

For this, long regarded as the English national dish, a good piece of beef sirloin is ideal. Less tender or smaller cuts will be improved by being cooked with a lid or a piece of foil over them for part of the time, and at slightly lower temperatures.

4 lb/2 kg/4 lb beef
a sprig of thyme

Wipe the meat and tie up if necessary, tucking the thyme and a piece of fat from the meat into the string on top of the joint. Place in a large roasting-tin near the top of a hot oven (400°F/200°C/Mark 6) for 30 minutes. Remove the tin, baste the meat with juice and fat from the tin, then replace at a lower heat (350°F/180°C/Mark 4) or in the lower half of the oven. Continue to cook allowing 20 minutes to the pound plus 20 minutes extra, for a medium roast; baste several times during cooking, and if the meat seems too dry put a piece of foil on top for the last 30 minutes. If you wish, potatoes may be roasted in the tin with the meat for about an hour before serving with gravy (see page 59), horseradish sauce (page 55) and green vegetables.

YORKSHIRE PUDDING

4 oz/125 g/1 cup flour
2 eggs
1/2 pt/300 ml/1 1/4 cups milk or milk
  and water

pinch salt
1 tbsp dripping or lard

Sift the flour and salt together into a bowl. Make a well in the flour and put in the eggs, then pour over half the milk. Beat well, leaving the sides of the bowl clean, then pour in the remaining milk and, if possible, allow the mixture to stand in a cool place for 30 minutes before beating further. Prepare either a shallow tin or some small patty tins by putting in the fat and allowing it to get hot for a few minutes. Beat the batter again and pour it into the hot tin; bake at the top of the oven for about 30 minutes until well risen and golden brown. Serve from the tin or cut into pieces and put around the joint on a large dish.

BEEFSTEAK AND KIDNEY PIE

Another old-fashioned dish that has remained very popular, this tastes best when the meat has been cooked slowly in the pie, but it

MEAT, POULTRY AND GAME

In the garden of Packwood Hall adjoining the church-
yard the borders were full of large clumps of single snow-
drops. I brought away a great bunch.

Juniper berries
(Juniperus
communis)

can be pre-cooked if time is short. Either way, use lean stewing beef, plenty of kidney and some mushrooms for an authentic flavour.

1½ lb/675 g/1½ lb beef
½ lb/225 g/½ lb ox kidney
1 onion
4 oz/125 g/1 cup sliced mushrooms
1 tsp chopped parsley
1 sprig thyme and 1 bay leaf

¼ tsp salt
a little ground black pepper
1 oz/25 g/2 tbsp dripping or butter
1 oz/25 g/¼ cup flour
½ pt/300 ml/1 cup gravy or stock or
* water*

Remove the core from the kidney and trim the fat off the beef. Cut the kidney into small slices and the beef into pieces about 1½ in (4 cm) long. Flour them, then melt the fat in a pan and fry the beef and kidney in it for about 5 minutes. Remove them and put them in a large pie-dish with the chopped onions and mushrooms. Sprinkle over the salt and pepper, add the herbs, and pour in the liquid; put in some extra stock or water, if needed, to come about ⅔ up the side of the pie-dish. Cover with puff or shortcrust pastry (see pages 85, 87) and brush over with beaten egg. Stand the dish in a shallow tin containing hot water, and cook in the lower half of a moderate oven (350°F/180°C/Mark 4) for about 2½ hours; cover the top with a piece of brown paper if the pastry seems likely to become too dark.

KIDNEY AND MUSHROOM CASSEROLE

1 lb/450 g/1 lb ox kidney
4 oz/125 g/1 cup sliced mushrooms
1 onion
½ pt/300 ml/1¼ cups stock or water
1 oz/25 g/2 tbsp butter or dripping
1 oz/25 g/¼ cup flour
salt and ground black pepper to
* taste*

pinch dried or sprig fresh rosemary
1 tbsp cream or 1 egg yolk
* (optional)*
a little grated nutmeg or lemon peel
* (optional)*

Melt the fat in a heavy pan or casserole. When hot, add the chopped onion and cook until browned. Wash, dry, skin and core the kidney and cut it into small pieces; sprinkle them with flour and add to the pan with the seasonings and herbs. Cook until the kidney is well browned, then add the sliced mushrooms and cook for 5 minutes longer. Pour in the hot stock, stirring until everything is mixed well. Transfer to a moderate oven (350°F/180°C/Mark 4) and cook covered for about 1 hour. Check that the meat is very tender, then add the cream or egg and the nutmeg or lemon. Stir well and serve hot. This dish may be served with green or root vegetables and boiled rice or potatoes; but it is perhaps best with spinach, and creamed potatoes.

MEAT, POULTRY AND GAME

Another day of bright sunshine. The leaf-buds in the hedges have been making wonderful progress these last three days of sunshine and the Elm blossom has opened out wide, showing all it's little anthers and filaments.

Juniper berries
(Juniperus
communis)

BRAISED BREAST OF VEAL

This is equally suitable for breast of mutton or lamb if veal is not available; mushroom stuffing may be used.

1 breast veal
stuffing, already mixed (see page 51)
1 oz/25 g/2 tbsp dripping or butter

2 onions
1 lb/450 g/1 lb carrots
1 small turnip or parsnip
1/2 pt/300 ml/1 1/4 cups water or stock

Bone the breast and remove as much surplus fat as possible. Spread the stuffing over it, then roll up and tie it with tape or string. Place the meat with the dripping in a heavy pan on the stove and brown on all sides. Remove from the pan and put it into a casserole on top of the cleaned and chopped vegetables. Pour in the hot stock, cover, and cook in moderate oven (350°F/180°C/Mark 4) for about 1 1/2 hours. Before serving, place the meat on a hot dish, or leave the lid off the casserole, so that it can brown.

LANCASHIRE HOT POT

There are many versions of this well-known North Country dish; the old recipe given here uses kidneys as well as the lamb or mutton chops which are always included. A straight-sided 'pot' is ideal for cooking this, but any casserole with a tight-fitting lid may be used.

2 lb/1 kg/2 lb lamb chops
2 lamb kidneys
4 oz/125 g/1/2 cup chopped lean bacon
4 oz/125 g/1 cup sliced mushrooms
3/4 lb/350 g/3/4 lb onions
3/4 lb/350 g/3/4 lb carrots

2 lb/1 kg/2 lb potatoes
1/2 pt/300 ml/1 1/4 cups water or stock
1/4 tsp mixed dried herbs or sprigs of thyme and parsley
1/4 tsp salt
ground pepper to taste
1 oz/25 g/2 tbsp butter

Trim the fat from the chops; skin and cut up the kidneys into small pieces. Wash and slice the carrots, but leave the mushrooms whole unless they are large; peel, wash and thinly slice the potatoes. Put the meat, bacon and vegetables in layers in the pot, beginning with the meat and finishing with a layer of potatoes; sprinkle herbs and seasonings between the layers and chop the butter into small pieces onto the final layer of potatoes. Pour in the stock, cover the pot, and cook in a slow oven (300°F/150°C/Mark 2) for about 3 hours. Take the lid off for the last 15 minutes to brown the potatoes a little, then serve straight from the pot. The cooking time can be reduced by about 30 minutes if the meat is first browned in a little fat, and the

There were numbers of flowers just opening; I only found one blossom fully expanded. The beds of white Violets and the bank where the white Periwinkle used to grow, that I had come to see, were some way off the road.

Juniper berries
(Juniperus
communis)

stock heated; but as with other dishes of this kind, slower cooking improves the flavour, and the hot pot may be cooked over a longer period if you wish.

LAMB WITH QUINCES OR CHESTNUTS

Cooking apples are often used in old-fashioned casseroles of lamb or mutton; the sharper flavour of quinces, however, makes this delicious.

2 lb/1 kg/2 lb best end neck of lamb   *¼ pt/150 ml/²/₃ cup water*
1 lb/500 g/1 lb quinces or chestnuts   *¼ tsp dried rosemary or marjoram*
   or cooking apples   *saltspoon each of salt and pepper*
1 oz/25 g/2 tbsp butter

Cut the lamb into chops, trimming off any surplus fat. Sprinkle with the herbs and seasonings and put with the water and butter into a casserole with a tight-fitting lid. Cook in a moderate oven (375°F/190°C/Mark 5) for about 45 minutes, then add the peeled and quartered quinces. Cook until the meat is tender and the fruit soft — about 1 hour — basting several times. If using chestnuts, boil them until they are soft, testing with a needle or skewer; then skin them and put them in the casserole about half-way through cooking the meat. Before serving leave the lid off for a few minutes to brown the meat and chestnuts, then serve with some gravy as the dish will be drier than when using quinces or apples.

SQUAB PIE

This is traditionally made with lamb chops and apples, with an onion added for a stronger flavour; use the same amounts as in the recipe for Lamb with Quinces, and substitute quinces for apples if you prefer. The pie will require

¾ lb/ 350 g/³/₄ lb of shortcrust pastry (see page 85).

In a large well buttered pie-dish put a layer of lamb chops, then one of sliced apples sprinkled with chopped onion, herbs and seasoning. Repeat until the dish is full and then pour in the water. Cover with the pastry and bake for 1½-2 hours in the lower half of a moderate oven (350°F/180°C/Mark 4). If the pastry seems to brown too quickly cover it with a piece of brown paper for the remaining cooking time.

A quick and sweeter version of this dish uses chopped cooked lamb or mutton together with apples, a few raisins and a sprinkling of brown sugar.

MEAT, POULTRY AND GAME

Among the notes of the numerous birds
I recognised those of the Thrush, Blackbird, Hedge Sparrow, Sky-lark,
Wren, Great Tit, Chaffinch, Green-finch, Pied Wagtail and Yellow Bunt-
ing. The latter was specially conspicious, perched up on top of the hedge

Juniper berries
(Juniperus
communis)

PORK IN CIDER

Cooking with cider is an old West Country speciality. A fairly dry kind is best for this dish, which can be made with pork chops if you prefer.

1 lb/450 g/1 lb pork fillet	1/4 pt/150 ml/2/3 cup cider or stock
1/2 lb/225 g/1/2 lb cooking apples	1/4 tsp ground cloves or 4 whole
1/2 lb/225 g/1/2 lb tomatoes	cloves
1 oz/25 g/ 2 tbsp butter	1/4 tsp ground black pepper
1 oz/25 g/1/4 cup demerara sugar	1/4 tsp salt

Place the sliced tomatoes with half the butter in the bottom of a casserole. Wipe and dry the meat, and cut it into neat cubes or slices; put this on top of the tomatoes, and sprinkle with salt and pepper. Peel, core and slice the apples and put these with the cloves on top of the pork; sprinkle the sugar over, dot with the remaining butter and pour in the cider. Cook in a moderate oven (350°F/180°C/ Mark 4) for about 2 hours. The cooking time can be reduced if the meat is cooked in melted butter before placing in the casserole, but the flavour is less delicate.

ROAST GOOSE

A well roasted goose makes a splendid alternative to the Christmas turkey, although tradition has it that the young bird tastes best in the autumn, at Michaelmas. The bird's giblets make a delicious stew, (see page 41); and it is a good idea to save the surplus fat, which is very good for cooking and as a preservative for cold meat. Plenty of fruit in the stuffing, and a good apple sauce, will help to counteract the richness of the bird. For the sage and onion stuffing, follow the basic recipe (page 51) and when mixing add the following:

2 large cooking apples, peeled and	1/4 tsp mustard powder
minced	1 tsp soft brown sugar
1/4 tsp ground cloves	

Alternatively make chestnut forcemeat (page 51); when mixing the cooked liver with the chestnuts add also:

1/2 lb/225 g/1 cup sausagemeat
2 sticks/1/2 cup chopped celery

Clean and dry the bird thoroughly, then stuff it and truss it for roasting. It may be wrapped in foil if you prefer and should be

MEAT, POULTRY AND GAME

After a wet, windy day, we woke this morning to a regular snow storm, the air was full of whirling flakes, but in the midst of it all I heard a Sky-lark singing.

Juniper berries
(Juniperus
communis)

basted well from time to time with the fat and juices; these will need spooning into a separate basin, since there is always a lot of fat from a goose. Allow 15 minutes cooking time for each 1 lb/450 g/1 lb of the bird's weight, plus 15 minutes over. Cook in a moderate oven (375°F/190°C/Mark 5).

FOR THE GRAVY:

giblets, neck and liver of goose
1 small onion
1 carrot
1 bay leaf
1/4 tsp salt
1 1/2 pt/850 ml/4 cups water
1 oz/25 g/1/4 cup flour

1 oz/25 g/2 tbsp butter or goose
 dripping
1/4 tsp ground nutmeg
1 tsp grated lemon or orange peel
salt and ground black pepper to
 taste

Put the giblets, neck and liver into a pan with the water, onion, carrot, bay leaf and salt. Bring to the boil, simmer for about 1 hour, then strain. Melt the fat in a saucepan, add the flour, and stir until they are well mixed. Pour in a little of the hot stock, stir, and add the remaining stock gradually. If you wish, add the sieved liver, then season the gravy with salt, pepper and nutmeg. Put in the lemon peel last, then reheat the gravy before serving. For apple sauce see page 55; roast potatoes, baked parsnips and buttered sprouts are good with goose.

GOOSE GIBLET STEW

goose giblets
2 onions
1 oz/25 g/1/4 cup flour
1 oz/25 g/2 tbsp butter or goose fat
1/2 lb/225 g/1/2 lb chestnuts (skinned)
1 pt/550 ml/2 1/2 cups goose stock

2 slices lemon or orange
2 cloves
1 clove of garlic
salt and ground black pepper
1 slice thick bread

Cover the giblets with stock, boil, skim well and add the cloves, garlic, orange and onions, chopped small. Melt half the fat in a pan, add the flour and when well mixed add a spoonful or two of the giblet stock, mixing carefully to avoid making it lumpy. As it thickens add one or two more spoonfuls of stock, then pour the mixture into the pan with the giblets. Bring to the boil again, stirring well, then cover the pan and simmer on a low heat for about 2 hours. Fry the bread in remaining goose fat, cut it into small squares and add these to the stew, together with the chestnuts (already baked or boiled till soft, and peeled). Cook together for a further 15 minutes

On the way home I found a Robin's nest in the bank of the lane. It was evidently just finished; This is the first finished nest I have seen this year.

Juniper berries
(Juniperus
communis)

with the lid off the pan, and serve with mashed potatoes or rice, and carrots or parsnips.

JUGGED HARE

Although young hare is good roasted, long slow cooking in a deep casserole is needed for the tougher meat of an older hare, which is also better hung for at least 24 hours. It may be soaked in a marinade to tenderize it if you wish, and for a rich gravy keep the blood to be added just before serving. Forcemeat balls are good with both hare and rabbit; these can be made from a simple parsley and thyme stuffing or a richer game stuffing (see page 53). Redcurrant or rowan jelly (page 121) usually completes the dish.

1 hare
4 oz/125 g/1/2 cup chopped lean
   bacon or ham
1 large onion
1 large carrot
2 sticks celery
2 oz/50 g/1/2 stick butter
1 oz/25 g/1/4 cup flour

1 1/2 tsp mixed dried herbs or sprigs
   thyme, parsley, marjoram
1/4 tsp ground nutmeg
salt and ground black pepper
1/2 pt/300 ml/1 1/4 cups beef or game
   stock (1 pt/600 ml/2 1/2 cups if no
   marinade is used)

FOR THE MARINADE:

1/4 pt/150 ml/2/3 cup red wine
2 tbsp lemon juice or wine vinegar
1 small onion
1/4 tsp ground cinnamon
1/4 tsp pepper

6 cloves
1 tsp soft brown sugar
1/4 tsp mixed dried herbs or sprigs
   thyme, parsley, marjoram
1 bay leaf

Clean, wash and cut up the hare; use the meatiest joints (shoulders, back, etc.) for the casserole, and the head with smaller pieces and bones to make stock or soup. If using the blood, drain this into a basin, adding a little brandy to stop it becoming too thick if it is to be kept for more than a few hours. Place the larger pieces of hare in a dish, sprinkle over the chopped onion, sugar, spices and seasonings then the wine and lemon juice mixed. Leave in this marinade overnight or longer, turning the pieces occasionally. Next day lift out the hare, dry well and flour it. Melt the butter in a heavy pan and fry the pieces gently until lightly browned; remove them to a deep casserole. Cook the bacon, sliced onion, chopped carrot and celery in the butter until soft, and put these in with the hare pieces. Pour over the strained marinade and the heated stock, then add the herbs, nutmeg and seasonings. Cover with a tight lid and cook in a

MEAT, POULTRY AND GAME

–the sun has brought out the green leaf-buds on the trees and hedges very rapidly, there is a marked difference in the Sycamore and Hawthorn the last few days, and the Larch is beginning to 'hang his tassels forth'.

Juniper berries
(Juniperus
communis)

slow oven (300°F/150°C/Mark 2) for at least 3 hours, until the meat is tender. If adding forcemeat balls, flour these lightly, fry them gently in a little fat for 5 minutes, then put them into the casserole. Cook for a further 30 minutes. If you wish to add the blood of the hare to the gravy, put it into a basin, pour in 2 tablespoonfuls of the cooking liquid, mix well; add some more liquid, stir, then return the mixture to the casserole or serve it in a separate gravy jug; but do not let the gravy overheat as it will curdle. The hare may be served straight from the casserole or on a dish with some gravy poured over it; a small glass of port is often stirred into the gravy, and redcurrant jelly adds sharpness to the strong flavour of the meat.

HUNTER'S PIE

This old recipe calls for an assortment of game and poultry, which may be varied according to preference and availability. Pheasant, hare and chicken pieces, for example, could be substituted for the whole game given here; and for a smaller pie use pieces rather than a whole rabbit or duck. Eggs, mushrooms and forcemeat are tasty additions to the pie; if it is to be served cold, shortcrust pastry is better, while either puff or flaky pastry is good for a hot pie. The recipe is also suitable for game casserole: add some more root vegetables before putting the pot into the oven, and cover the meat with thinly sliced potatoes dotted with butter.

1 partridge	*¹/₂ tsp salt*
1 rabbit	*¹/₄ tsp ground black pepper*
1 wild duck	*¹/₄ tsp ground cloves or nutmeg*
2 onions	*¹/₄ tsp mixed dried herbs or sprigs*
1 carrot	*marjoram, thyme, parsley*
1 stick celery	*1 bay leaf*
2 oz/50 g/¹/₂ stick butter	*1 pt/600 ml/2¹/₂ cups game or beef*
1 oz/25 g/¹/₄ cup flour	*stock*

Clean, wash and dry the birds and rabbit; truss or, if large, halve or joint the birds; joint the rabbit, and keep back the smaller pieces and head for stock. Flour all the meat well, then lightly brown it in the melted butter in a large heavy pan. Put the sliced onions, carrot and celery in the bottom of a large casserole, sprinkle them with a little salt and pepper, and put the pieces of meat on top. Add the heated stock, seasonings and herbs, then cook in a fairly slow oven (325°F/160°C/Mark 3) for 2-3 hours. When tender, remove the meat from the bones, and arrange it in layers in a large pie-dish with the

MEAT, POULTRY AND GAME

Another glorious day. Cycled to Knowle, On the way found some Marsh
Marigolds and Black thorn in blossom. The Tadpoles have come
out of their balls of jelly and career madly about the aquarium wag-
=ging their little black tails.

Juniper berries.
(Juniperus
communis)

sliced eggs and forcemeat. Fill up with stock from the casserole, cover with pastry and bake in a moderately hot oven (375°F/190°C/ Mark 5) for 45 minutes, or until the top is golden brown.

GROUSE ON TOAST

This is a very old-fashioned simple way of serving grouse, but it should be young and well hung. The breast only of the bird is eaten, but the liver can be fried and spread on toast or mixed with the gravy if you wish. Redcurrant, cranberry or rowan jelly are good with this and other game, and watercress, if available, is the best garnish, having a stronger flavour than parsley.

2 grouse
2 large slices of streaky bacon
1 oz/25 g/¹/₄ cup flour

2 oz/50 g/4 tbsp butter or dripping
2 slices toast

Clean, wipe and truss the grouse, tucking a slice of bacon under the string to cover the breast of each bird. Put them in a roasting tin with the fat in a very hot oven (450°F/230°C/Mark 8) for about 20 minutes, basting often with the fat and gravy. When tender remove the bacon and dredge the birds with the flour; continue to roast and baste them until they are well browned. Toast the bread, spoon gravy from the pan on each slice and serve the grouse on the toast while still very hot.

STEWED VENISON CUTLETS

The cutlets from the best end of neck of venison are used for this dish, which is good for a smaller quantity of meat, and for slices of venison steak if you prefer not to grill them.

2 lb/1 kg/2 lb venison
2 oz/50 g/¹/₂ stick butter
¹/₄ pt/150 ml/²/₃ cup red wine
¹/₂ pt/300 ml/1¹/₄ cups stock
3 shallots or 1 small onion, chopped
2 oz/50 g/¹/₂ cup sliced mushrooms

salt and ground black pepper to
taste
¹/₄ tsp ground nutmeg
1 tbsp chopped parsley or sprigs of
watercress

Trim and wipe the cutlets, and put them in a heavy pan with the butter and onion. Fry until browned, then add the mushrooms and cook for a few minutes longer. Pour the wine over the meat, and let it heat, then add the hot stock, nutmeg and seasoning to taste. Simmer gently for about 45 minutes. Garnish, and serve with peas or beans and creamed potatoes.

POTTED GAME

4 oz/125 g/¹/₂ cup cooked game
4 oz/125 g/¹/₂ cup boiled ham or
* bacon*
¹/₂ tsp mushroom ketchup or
* Worcester sauce*

edge tsp each of ground allspice,
* mace, black pepper, salt*
1 oz/25 g/2 tbsp butter

Make sure that the meat is free of bone, skin or excess fat, then either mince or pound it all to a fine paste, adding the seasonings very gradually until they are well blended. If necessary sieve the mixture then put it into small pots or jars. These should be sterilized as for jam. Cover the mixture with a thick layer of melted clarified butter, then keep in a cool place until needed. A mixture of ham and chicken or other poultry is also good, and chopped parsley can be added to the paste when used.

LIVER PÂTÉ

¹/₂ lb/225 g/¹/₂ lb lambs' liver
1-2 tbsp chopped onion
2-3 tbsp cream or white sauce
1 egg yolk
2 tsp chopped parsley or chives

¹/₄ tsp ground nutmeg
salt and ground black pepper
1 oz/25 g/2 tbsp butter or margarine
1 tbsp flour

Wipe the liver, flour and season it lightly, then cook it gently in a saucepan or frying-pan with the melted butter and the onion. When it is lightly browned, remove and cool the liver. Mince or pound it, then put it through the mincer a second time with the onion and parsley. Season it well with the nutmeg, salt and pepper, add the sauce or cream and the egg yolk; mix well, season again to taste, and place the mixture in a greased tin or dish. Cover with greased paper and stand it in a pan of hot water either in the oven (300°F/150°C/Mark 2) or on gentle heat, for about 30 minutes. Cool and turn out the pâté onto a bed of lettuce.

4 STUFFINGS AND SAUCES

Crab·apple (Pyrus malus)
and
White·throat

STUFFINGS AND SAUCES

Travelled down to Stoke Bishop near Bristol. The low-lying fertile lands round the Avon in Worcestershire were golden with Marsh Marigolds, and as we went through Gloucestershire the banks were starred with Primroses and I saw a good many Cowslips. The Plum and Damson trees were all in blossom.

Crab-apple (*Pyrus malus*)

STUFFINGS AND SAUCES

It is often the 'extras' such as sauces or stuffings that give a dish its special character, so it is worth spending time on their preparation. Some of the most popular are also the easiest, and these are given here, together with others perhaps less familiar.

SAGE AND ONION STUFFING

A classic stuffing, used with pork, duck or goose.

1 lb/450 g/1 lb onions
4 oz/125 g/2 cups soft breadcrumbs
1 tsp dried or 1 tbsp finely chopped
  fresh sage

½ tsp salt
¼ tsp ground black pepper

Quarter the peeled onions, and cook them in slightly salted boiling water for 10-15 minutes, until tender. Remove and chop or mash them, then add them to the dry ingredients, mixing well. Use a little of the cooking liquid or melted butter to bind if the stuffing is too dry. A more substantial stuffing is made by adding 1-2 tablespoons of suet, and a beaten egg to bind.

CHESTNUT FORCEMEAT

For roast fowl or turkey.

½ lb/225 g/½ lb chestnuts
liver of fowl or turkey
2 oz/50 g/¼ cup chopped lean ham
  or bacon
1 oz/25 g/2 tbsp chopped onion
1 oz/25 g/2 tbsp butter

1 egg yolk
2 tbsp stock (from chestnuts or liver)
2 oz/50 g/1 cup soft breadcrumbs
1 tsp chopped parsley
½ tsp salt
¼ tsp pepper

Slit the chestnuts, boil or bake for 15 minutes, then peel them. Cook them for 20 minutes in boiling water or stock to cover, then remove them from the pan, pound or mash them in a basin. Finely chop the liver, or mash it with a fork if it is already cooked, and mix it with the chestnuts. Put in the onion, bacon and breadcrumbs, then add the parsley and seasonings. Melt the butter in a small pan, add the egg yolk, and mix with the stock; then use this mixture to bind together the dry ingredients in the basin.

MUSHROOM STUFFING

Very good with roast turkey.

4 oz/125 g/¼ lb mushrooms
1 oz/25 g/2 tbsp butter
1 small onion

2 oz/50 g/¼ cup chopped bacon
1 tsp lemon juice
4 oz/125 g/2 cups soft breadcrumbs

STUFFINGS AND SAUCES

Painted the pony and colt all morning in the field
Very hot sun and cool breeze. Saw a beautiful Peacock
butterfly and found some Purple Orchis in flower.

Crab apple (Pyrus malus)

1 egg yolk   *ground black pepper*
¹/₄ tsp salt

Wash the mushrooms in cold water; the stalks and skin can be left on if they are fresh and tender. Without drying them, place them in a pan with the butter, chopped onion, bacon and lemon juice. Cover the pan and stew gently over low heat until very soft. Lift out the mushrooms and mash or chop them, then add them, with the remaining contents of the pan, to the breadcrumbs. Mix well, and add the beaten egg yolk; put in a second yolk if the mixture appears too dry. Season well with salt and pepper.

LIVER AND BACON STUFFING

This rich stuffing is very suitable for use with game, and for cold meat dishes such as galantines or pies. The mixture also makes a good pâté, using double quantities and baked in the oven.

8 oz/250 g/¹/₂ lb calves' liver
2 oz/50 g/1 cup soft breadcrumbs
4 oz/125 g/¹/₂ cup chopped streaky bacon
2 oz/50 g/¹/₂ cup chopped onion
1 oz/25 g/2 tbsp butter

¹/₂ tsp mixed dried herbs or 1 tsp chopped parsley and a sprig of thyme
1 egg yolk or ¹/₂ a beaten egg
¹/₄ tsp salt
a shake of pepper

Chop the liver very small, then put in a pan with the butter, onion, and bacon. Cook quickly for a minute or two, then cover the pan and cook gently over a low heat for about 20 minutes until the mixture is very soft, stirring occasionally to prevent sticking. When cooked cool the mixture a little before mixing it with the breadcrumbs, seasoning and herbs. Bind together with the egg, adding a little stock or more egg if the mixture is too dry.

BREAD SAUCE

A traditional accompaniment to the Christmas turkey, this is also good with pheasant and other game.

4 oz/125 g/2 cups soft white breadcrumbs
1 onion
6 whole cloves
³/₄ pt/450 ml/2 cups milk

¹/₄ tsp salt
ground black pepper or nutmeg
¹/₂ oz/15 g/1 tbsp butter or 1 tbsp thick cream

Stick the cloves into the peeled onion and place it in a pan with the milk; heat this till near boiling point, then remove from heat and

STUFFINGS AND SAUCES

Another brilliant day. Saw a pair of House Martins, watched some Trout in the Leet and found a Chaffinch's nest nearly finished in a young Hawthorn.

Crab-apple (*Pyrus malus*)

allow to stand, still keeping it warm, for about 10 minutes. Then lift out the onion, and add the breadcrumbs and salt to the milk; stir well. Replace the onion, and leave in the sauce for a further 10-15 minutes; before serving, remove the onion, stir the butter or cream into the sauce, and add some freshly ground black pepper or nutmeg to taste.

APPLE SAUCE

For roast or grilled pork, roast goose, and fried or grilled pork sausages.

8 oz/225 g/½ lb cooking apples *½ oz/15 g/1 tbsp soft brown sugar*
½ oz/15 g/1 tbsp butter *water*

Peel and slice the apples, and place in a pan with enough water to cover the bottom of the pan. Cook very gently over low heat until the apples are soft; remove from heat and add the sugar and butter, stirring well. Serve either hot or cold, adding a sprinkling of ground cinnamon or cloves if you like a spicy flavour.

MINT SAUCE

Useful for any roast or grilled lamb, or with mutton, this is best made several hours before it is needed.

2 tbsp finely chopped fresh mint *1 tbsp hot water*
2 tsp castor sugar (fine sugar) *2 tbsp malt vinegar*

In a small jug or basin, dissolve the sugar in the hot water. Stir in the mint and leave until cold; then stir in the vinegar and leave to stand before serving. Mint sauce will keep well in an airtight bottle or jar, but the water should be omitted; instead, add a further tablespoonful of vinegar and a little salt to the above amounts of mint and sugar. When needed, add a little cold water before serving.

HORSERADISH SAUCE

Usually served with roast beef, this is also good with fried or grilled herring or mackerel and can be stored for several days if required.

1 tbsp grated horseradish *1 tbsp double cream*
¼ tsp castor sugar (fine sugar) *a pinch of salt and a pinch of*
1 large tsp malt vinegar *mustard powder*

Pink Campion in bloom. Walking through the fields, came upon quite a grove of young Cherry-trees in blossom, growing all along the top of one of the banks.

Crab-apple (Pyrus malus)

Mix the dry ingredients together, then add the cream and vinegar; stir well and add a little milk if you prefer a thinner sauce. It can be served hot as well as cold, but should be heated gently in a basin over hot water.

HOLLANDAISE SAUCE

Suitable for veal and any fish, but specially good with hot salmon.

2 egg yolks
1 tbsp water
strained juice of ½ lemon

1 tbsp cream
salt and ground black pepper to
 taste

Whisk together the egg yolks and water with a fork. Stand the basin in a pan of hot water over a low heat, and add the cream and seasoning, stirring well all the time. Keep hot and serve hot, but do not allow to boil, or the sauce will curdle.

WHITE SAUCE

This basic recipe, with a variety of additions, can be used either for fish or meat, or with vegetable dishes; stock from these may be used instead of, or mixed with, milk.

1 oz/25 g/¼ cup flour
1 oz/25 g/2 tbsp butter

½ pt/300 ml/1¼ cups milk or stock

In a heavy saucepan, melt the butter, but do not let it brown. Heat, but do not boil, the liquid. Add the flour to the butter, stirring until they are well mixed, then add the liquid a little at a time, stirring to keep the sauce smooth. When all the liquid is added, bring to the boil, then simmer for a further 5 minutes. Remove from heat, and put in the required flavourings. Sometimes these additions may make the sauce thicker than required, in which case a little more warmed liquid may be added. Season with salt and pepper to taste. Garnishes such as parsley should be added as near as possible to the time of serving, and care should always be taken when adding lemon or eggs, which can easily curdle the the sauce.

ANCHOVY SAUCE

Add 1 tsp anchovy essence, ½ tsp lemon juice, cayenne pepper to taste.

EGG SAUCE

Add 1 chopped hard-boiled egg, cayenne pepper or ground nutmeg to taste.

STUFFINGS AND SAUCES

Here the Gorse and Blackthorn blossom was very fine and in the bogs we found Marsh Violets and the Small Water Crowfoot but there are very few of the bog-flowers out as yet.

Crab-apple (Pyrus malus)

MUSHROOM SAUCE

Add 2-4 tbsp chopped mushrooms, ½ tsp lemon juice.

ONION SAUCE

Add 1 finely chopped small onion, ground nutmeg or black pepper to taste.

PARSLEY SAUCE

Add 1-2 tbsp chopped parsley, a small knob of butter.

MUSTARD SAUCE

Add 1-2 tsp made mustard powder, ½ tsp brown sugar, cayenne pepper to taste.

CHEESE SAUCE

Add 2-4 tbsp grated Cheddar cheese, ground nutmeg or cayenne pepper to taste.

GRAVY FOR ROAST MEAT

This is tastiest made using surplus fat from the joint or bird, in the pan in which it was roasted; but it may be made with dripping or butter in a saucepan if preferred. Use flour, fat and liquid in the same proportions as for white sauce, and meat or vegetable stock instead of milk. Season well, and strain into a hot jug to serve.

MAYONNAISE

This basic recipe can be used plain or with additions such as the following:

2 tsp chopped fresh herbs (chives, basil, marjoram, burnet, lemon balm) or	*1 tsp minced onion or shallot or 1 chopped gherkin together with 1 tsp chopped parsley*

For a richer sauce, add 1 tbsp cream, with a little ground nutmeg, cinnamon or cayenne pepper.

2 egg yolks	*¼ pt/150 ml/⅔ cup olive oil*
¼ tsp salt	*1 tbsp wine or tarragon vinegar or*
¼ tsp mustard powder	*lemon juice*
a pinch of freshly ground pepper	

Mix the egg yolks and seasonings together in a bowl. Beat until smooth, then add the oil, a teaspoon at a time at first, stirring

STUFFINGS AND SAUCES

In the afternoon went to Huckworthy Bridge that spans the river Walkham. Down hill all the way. In the meadows beside the river I was surprised to find the blue Alkanet already in blossom just where I found it in July last year.

Crab·apple (Pyrus malus)

quickly to blend it in well, and as it thickens increasing the addition of oil. When all the oil is smoothly mixed in, add the vinegar or lemon juice gradually and mix to a thick cream. Other additions such as herbs or cream should be added last, and thoroughly mixed in.

SIMPLE SALAD DRESSING

1 tbsp olive oil
juice of 1 small lemon

1 tsp chopped basil, chives or
parsley
salt and pepper to taste

Mix together very well, and use as a light dressing for a green or tomato salad.

Sweet sauces can make even the simplest sponge pudding seem interesting, and they are very good with ice-cream or blancmange.

SWEET MELTED BUTTER

¹/₂ oz/15 g/1tbsp butter
¹/₂ oz/15 g/2 tbsp flour
¹/₂ pt/300 ml/1¹/₄ cups water

1 oz/25 g/3 tbsp castor sugar (fine
sugar)
¹/₄ tsp ground cinnamon

In a heavy pan, stir the butter and flour together over a low heat till smooth. Gradually add the warmed water, stirring well; bring to the boil, and stir until the sauce thickens. Remove from heat and add the sugar and cinnamon; serve hot, either poured over the pudding or in a small jug.

CUSTARD SAUCE

2 eggs
1 oz/25 g/3 tbsp sugar
¹/₂ pt/300 ml/1¹/₄ cups milk

a few drops vanilla essence or a
little grated lemon or orange rind

Beat the eggs and sugar together in a basin. Heat the milk to just below boiling point, then pour into the egg mixture. Whisk well, add the flavouring, and return to the pan; stir over a gentle heat until the sauce thickens but do not boil. Serve hot, with boiled suet puddings or steamed sponge puddings. The same mixture makes an excellent baked custard, cooked in a greased dish for about 40 minutes in a moderate oven (350°F/180°F/Mark 4).

JAM SAUCE

A simple sauce for sponge puddings.

1 tbsp jam (raspberry, apricot,   *¹/4 pt/150 ml/²/3 cup water*
*   plum, etc.)*   *1 tsp lemon juice*
1 tbsp sugar

Put the sugar, jam and water in a heavy pan, and bring to the boil. Cook quickly for about 10 minutes, add the lemon juice, and pour over the pudding before serving.

RICH ORANGE SAUCE

1 white and 2 yolks of egg   *juice of 2 oranges*
3 oz/75 g/3 oz granulated sugar   *1 tbsp lemon juice*
grated rind of 1 orange

Beat the eggs together in a bowl, then beat in the sugar gradually. Stand the bowl in a pan of hot water on a low heat; stir in the strained juice and the orange rind a little at a time, letting the sauce thicken like custard. Remove when it is a good pouring consistency, and serve at once in a warm jug or bowl, with steamed sponge pudding or with ice-cream.

MOLASSES SAUCE

This is good with apple dumplings or boiled suet puddings; golden syrup may be used instead of molasses if preferred.

6 oz/175 g/¹/2 cup molasses or   *¹/2 oz/15 g/1 tbsp butter*
*   golden syrup*   *2 tsp lemon juice*

Boil all the ingredients together for about 15 minutes in a heavy pan, then pour over the pudding and serve.

BRANDY BUTTER

This is traditionally served, either with or without custard sauce, with plum pudding at Christmas.

4 oz/125 g/1 stick butter   *2-3 tbsp brandy*
3 oz/75 g/3 oz castor sugar (fine
*   sugar)*

Cream the butter and sugar together until very soft. Beat in the brandy a little at a time so that the mixture is light and smooth; serve chilled in a glass dish. Rum butter is made in the same way, but soft brown sugar is used instead of white sugar; add ¹/2 tsp of lemon juice if liked.

5 *EGGS AND SAVOURIES*

Fruit
of
Wild Guelder Rose
(Viburnum opulus)

EGGS AND SAVOURIES

We walked four miles through the woods to Plym Bridge at the far end of the Vale. A Water Ouzel skimmed across the river and in under the arch·way of the old, grey, stone bridge, every cranny of which was green with tiny ferns.

Hips of Villous Rose
(Rosa villosa).

EGGS AND SAVOURIES

Eggs have long been regarded as the cook's standby for the production of quick yet satisfying dishes. Many good recipes for these have been neglected and are worth reviving, while even such favourites as poached eggs can be varied in interesting ways.

ANCHOVY POACHED EGGS

4 eggs
4 rounds of toast
1 oz/25 g/2 tbsp butter
4 tsp anchovy essence

4 tsp chopped parsley
1/2 tsp salt
1/2 tsp lemon juice

Half fill a saucepan with water, bring it to the boil and add the salt and lemon juice. Break each egg into a saucer, then poach them in the water, which should simmer gently. When they are set remove each egg to a piece of toast prepared as follows: lightly toast each slice on both sides, butter well, and sprinkle a teaspoonful of anchovy essence over each so that it blends with the butter; prick the toast with a fork so that the butter and essence soak in; keep hot until the eggs are ready. Then top each poached egg with a small piece of butter and a spoonful of parsley. For a change, substitute a large teaspoonful of finely grated cheese for the anchovy essence, and sprinkle the tops of the eggs with chopped chives.

SCOTCH EGGS

1/2 lb/225 g/1 cup sausagemeat
4 oz/125 g/2 cups soft breadcrumbs
1 tbsp chopped parsley
1/4 tsp salt
ground black pepper

1 beaten egg
4 hard-boiled eggs
1-2 tbsp fine dry breadcrumbs
lard or dripping

Mix together with a fork the sausagemeat, soft breadcrumbs, parsley and seasonings. Bind them with half the beaten egg and divide the mixture into four. Shell the hard-boiled eggs, and cover each with a portion of the sausage mixture, using floured hands to flatten and shape the mixture round the eggs. Dip each one into the remaining beaten egg and then into the dry breadcrumbs; fry the eggs in hot lard or dripping until golden brown, drain, and serve hot with tomato sauce or cold with salad.

Watched the sun set behind the hills, from the top of Yanna=
=don Down. Gorgeous gold and purple clouds, near the horizon
and up above, clear golden sky!

Hips of Villous Rose
(Rosa villosa).

EGG AND HAM SAVOURIES

Cooked tongue or chicken can be used instead of ham.

4 eggs
4 oz/125 g/¹/₂ cup minced cooked
* ham*

1 oz/25 g/¹/₄ cup minced parsley
1 oz/25 g/2 tbsp butter

Use a little butter to grease 4 small baking dishes or moulds. Sprinkle into each first the minced ham, then the parsley. Break an egg into each dish, place a piece of butter on top of each egg, and place the dishes in a larger tin containing enough hot water to come half-way up the dishes. Bake in a moderate oven (350°F/180°C/Mark 4) for about 15 minutes or until the eggs are well set. Either serve the eggs in the dishes, or lift them out onto rounds of buttered toast or fried bread. Garnish with a little cayenne pepper.

EGGS AND PARSLEY

4 eggs
¹/₂ pt/300 ml/1¹/₄ cups white sauce
1 oz/25 g/¹/₄ cup grated cheese or 2
* tbsp minced ham*

1 tbsp minced parsley
salt and pepper to taste

Make the basic white sauce (see page 57) and keep it hot. Boil the eggs for 5 minutes, shell them as soon as possible, and cut a slice off the white of each so that it can stand on end. Butter 4 small serving dishes and place an egg on each; add the chopped up slices of egg white and the parsley to the white sauce, season and pour this round each egg. Sprinkle grated cheese or minced ham over each egg, top with a small piece of butter, and place the dishes in a hot oven or under a grill for a few minutes before serving.

BACON AND EGG PIE

6 oz/175 g/6 oz lean bacon rashers
3 eggs
¹/₄ pt/150 ml/²/₃ cup milk
salt and pepper

a little grated nutmeg
³/₄ lb/350 g/³/₄ lb shortcrust pastry
* (see page 85)*

Divide the pastry into two and use one half to line a greased 9-10 in (24 cm) tin or plate. Chop the bacon into 1 in (2 cm) pieces and fry it lightly in a very little butter. Allow it to cool while whisking the eggs and milk together in a bowl. Add the seasonings and nutmeg to taste. Arrange the bacon on top of the pastry, then pour over the egg and milk mixture so that it fills but does not overflow the plate.

EGGS AND SAVOURIES

A native of Dousland showed me a bank covered with gorse and briars, where he said he was sure a Bramble Finch was building, I only know this bird by reputation; so mean to go again and watch for it.

Hips of Villous Rose
(Rosa villosa).

Moisten the edges and cover the pie with the second half of the pastry, pressing firmly along the edges, which can be fluted between thumb and finger or lightly pressed with a fork; do not fork over the top of the pie. Glaze lightly with a little egg and milk, then bake in a moderate oven (350°F/180°C/Mark 4) for about 35 minutes until lightly browned. Individual bacon and egg tarts, baked in patty tins, can also be made in the same way.

KIDNEY OMELETTE

This makes a good breakfast or lunch dish.

1 sheep's kidney
2 eggs
1 oz/25 g/2 tbsp butter

½ tsp chopped chives or parsley
salt and pepper to taste

Wash and skin the kidney; chop it into small pieces and fry it in half the butter in a small heavy pan. Drain and leave it to cool. Beat the eggs together very lightly with a fork, add the seasonings and kidney; melt the remaining butter in a heavy frying-pan, and when it is hot but not brown, pour in the omelette mixture. Cook this until it begins to set, then loosen the edges with a knife, fold over, and serve on a hot dish. Chives or parsley may be used as a garnish, or cooked in the omelette with the kidney.

CHEESE CUSTARDS

4 eggs
1 pt/550 ml/2½ cups milk
1 oz/25 g/2 tbsp butter
2 oz/50 g/½ cup finely grated cheese

¼ tsp salt
¼ tsp white and cayenne pepper mixed
pinch bicarbonate of soda (baking soda)

Beat the eggs in a large bowl. Bring the milk to the boil, then pour it into the eggs. Stirring quickly, add the cheese, seasonings and bicarbonate of soda; pour the mixture into well buttered moulds or small baking dishes and stir to prevent the cheese from sinking to the bottom. Stand them in a baking tin containing enough hot water to reach more than half-way up the moulds, and bake in a moderate oven (350°F/180°C/Mark 4) until well set. Garnish with parsley.

The Cuckoo has been heard long ago in other parts of the county, but up here on the moors we have not yet heard it.

Hips of Villous Rose
(Rosa villosa).

CHEESE SCALLOPS

2 oz/50 g/1 cup soft breadcrumbs
1/2 pt/300 ml/1 1/4 cups milk
1 beaten egg
3 oz/75 g/3/4 cup grated cheese

1 oz/25 g/2 tbsp butter
2 oz/50 g/1/2 cup dry breadcrumbs
1/4 tsp cayenne pepper
1/4 tsp salt

Soak the soft breadcrumbs in the warm milk in a basin. Mix in the egg, cheese, salt and cayenne, and half the butter melted. With the rest of the butter, grease four scallop shells and shake half the dry breadcrumbs into them. Put some of the cheese mixture into each shell and sprinkle the rest of the dry breadcrumbs over the mixture. Bake the scallops for 20-30 minutes in a fairly hot oven (400°F/ 200°C/Mark 6) until golden brown; serve from the shells, very hot, as a first course or light lunch dish.

WELSH RABBIT

This favourite savoury is best served very hot, with plenty of mustard or pepper added when mixing.

4 oz/125 g/1 cup grated strong
  cheese
1 egg

2-3 tbsp milk
1/2 tsp mustard powder
2 thick slices toast

Butter the toast well and keep it hot. Place the cheese in a small heavy pan, break in the egg, add the milk and mustard powder and stir well over moderate heat until the mixture boils. Pour it quickly over the slices of toast and serve at once. Some old versions of this dish suggest ale or red wine in place of the egg and milk, with cheese and butter added to the heated liquid.

HAM TOAST

This makes a good savoury alternative to cheese on toast.

4 oz/125 g/1/2 cup minced cooked
  ham
1 chopped gherkin (optional)
2 beaten eggs or 1/4 pt/150 ml/
  2/3 cup white sauce

1/4 tsp mustard powder
salt and pepper to taste
2 thick slices toast

Mix together in a basin the ham, gherkin, seasonings and eggs or sauce. Butter the toast well, place it on an ovenproof dish and pour the ham mixture over each slice. Put the dish into a hot oven (425°F/ 220°C/Mark 7) for about 15 minutes until browned; serve very hot.

TOAD-IN-THE-HOLE

This well known dish is usually made with sausages, but is also delicious made with meat, as in the following recipe.

12 oz/350 g/1½ cups minced *2 or 3 tomatoes, sliced*
  cooked ham, or beef, or chicken *1 tbsp chopped parsley*
1 chopped onion *salt and pepper to taste*

FOR THE BATTER:

½ oz/15 g/1 tbsp butter or dripping *½ pt/300 ml/1¼ cups milk or milk*
4 oz/125 g/1 cup self-raising flour *and water*
¼ tsp salt *1 large egg*

Sift the flour and salt together into a bowl and make a well in the middle of the flour. Break the egg into this, then pour in half the milk, beating well so that the mixture leaves the sides of the bowl. Pour over the remaining milk, and leave in a cool place for at least 30 minutes if possible, as this helps to give a lighter batter. Grease a pie-dish with the butter or dripping and put into it the meat, onion and tomatoes, sprinkled with parsley and seasonings. Place it in a hot oven (425°F/220°C/Mark 7) for 5 minutes while finishing the batter. Beat this well so that the milk is thoroughly mixed in, remove the dish from the oven and pour the batter into it; replace it quickly and bake for about 45 minutes, until well risen and golden brown. Serve with gravy and green vegetables.

SAUSAGE TOAD

Prepare the batter as for toad-in-the-hole, but use either pork or beef sausages instead of meat.

1 lb/450 g/1 lb skinned sausages *1 oz/25 g/2 tbsp dripping or lard*
1 small chopped onion (optional)

Place the sausages, onion and dripping in a pie-dish and put this in a hot oven (425°F/220°C/Mark 7) for 5 minutes, until well heated. Remove and pour over the batter and bake as in the previous recipe.

6 *VEGETABLE DISHES AND SALADS*

Honeysuckle
(*Lonicera caprifolium*)

VEGETABLE DISHES AND SALADS

In Somerset the meadows were yellow with cowslips, these flowers are not found in Devon, except on the northern borders of the county; farmers will tell you the soil is 'too good' for them.

Wild Pear (Pyrus Communis)

VEGETABLE DISHES AND SALADS

Towards the end of the nineteenth century increasing interest was shown in the use of vegetables, not merely as 'extras' but as tasty and economical meals on their own. Recipes for these appeared not only in books of vegetarian cookery but in everyday cookbooks and pamphlets too.

CELERY CHEESE

1 large head celery
3/4 pt/450 ml/ 2 cups cheese sauce
 (see page 59)
2 oz/50 g/1/2 cup grated strong
 cheese

2 oz/50 g/1/2 cup fine dry
 breadcrumbs
2 hard-boiled eggs
1/2 oz/15 g/1 tbsp butter

Clean the celery stalks and chop into small pieces, reserving the leaves for garnish. Put enough lightly salted water into a large saucepan to cover the bottom of the pan, and steam the celery gently in this until it is tender. When it is cooked put it into an ovenproof dish and keep it hot. Make the sauce (see page 59) using for this any liquid left from cooking the celery. Pour the hot sauce over the celery, arrange the sliced eggs over it then sprinkle over the breadcrumbs mixed with the grated cheese, dot with butter and place in a hot oven or under a grill for a few minutes to brown lightly. Garnish the dish with celery leaves before serving.

LEEK PIE

This has long been a popular dish, being simple to make and very tasty. Young tender leeks are best, for then the green as well as the white part can be used.

1 lb/450 g/1 lb leeks
1 pt/550 ml/2 1/2 cups white sauce
6 oz/175 g/1 1/2 cups grated strong
 cheese

4 oz/125 g/1 cup dry breadcrumbs
2 oz/50 g/1/2 stick butter

Wash the leeks very thoroughly and cut off the roots. Chop the leeks to about 3 in (7 cm) lengths, cover them with salted water in a saucepan and simmer for about 20 minutes or until tender. Make a white sauce (see page 57) using cooking liquid from the leeks if you wish. Butter a pie-dish and put the leeks in this in layers with the sauce, cheese and breadcrumbs. Top the pie with a layer of breadcrumbs, then grated cheese, and dot with pieces of butter; bake in a moderate oven (350°F/180°C/Mark 4) until well browned. For a change the pie can be topped with slices of streaky bacon or

Warm south west wind, with heavy fall of rain. Gathered some wild Pear blossom and the first 'Cow-slips I have picked this year. Saw two hen Blackbirds sitting on their nests, — one in a hollow tree.

Wild Pear (*Pyrus Communis*)

tomatoes. Other vegetables such as marrow, broccoli and tomatoes can be baked in the same way; or try a mixture of root vegetables, such as carrot, parsnip and kohl-rabi.

MUSHROOM PUDDING

1 lb/450 g/1 lb field mushrooms   *3 oz/75 g/³⁄₄ stick butter*
¹⁄₂ lb/225 g/2 cups flour   *salt and pepper to taste*
2 oz/50 g/1 cup soft breadcrumbs

Mix flour with breadcrumbs and a little salt, rub in the butter, adding enough water to moisten; roll out the mixture and line a greased pudding basin with it. Peel the mushrooms, slicing them if they are large, and pile them in the centre together with the butter and water. Season to taste. Cover with a lid of the breadcrumb pastry, place a piece of greased paper on top and steam the pudding for about 1¹⁄₂ hours. Chopped onion or tomato may be added if you like and sprinkling the mushrooms with a little freshly grated nutmeg makes them extra tasty.

PARSNIP CAKES

Parsnips are a very versatile and nourishing, but somewhat neglected, vegetable. This recipe is useful when there are large parsnips available.

4 large parsnips   *2 oz/50 g/¹⁄₂ cup dry breadcrumbs*
1 tsp flour   *a little milk*
1 egg   *salt and ground black pepper*

Scrub the parsnips well and cook them in fast-boiling salted water until they are tender. Drain them and either mash with a potato masher or rub them through a coarse sieve until they are smooth. Mix in the flour, beaten egg and plenty of salt and pepper; form the mixture into round flat cakes 3-4 in (7-8 cm) across, dip these in milk and breadcrumbs then fry them in shallow butter or dripping till brown on both sides. The cakes are delicious served very hot with a green salad. This recipe can also be used for other root vegetables such as carrot or swede.

COLCANNON

Although this dish is often made with cabbage, young kale gives a better flavour; bubble-and-squeak is another version of the dish,

VEGETABLE DISHES AND SALADS

I saw a pair of White-throats today down Widney lane, they were evid-ently rivals, and were chasing each other through the bushes, singing loudly all the time. By the Blythe I saw a very handsome pair of Black-headed Buntings.

Wild Pear (.Pyrus Communis)

and should contain chopped meat or bacon, though it is often made without.

8 oz/225 g/$^1/_2$ lb mashed cooked
   potato
8 oz/225 g/$^1/_2$ lb cooked kale or
   cabbage

1 small onion
1 oz/25 g/2 tbsp dripping
salt and pepper
1 oz/25 g/2 tbsp dry breadcrumbs

Chop the kale and mix it with the potato; season well. Melt the dripping in a pan and cook the chopped onion until it is soft; add the potato and kale mixture, and toss until it is well heated. It can then be browned and served straight from the pan, but it can instead be put into a greased basin well sprinkled with breadcrumbs; press the mixture firmly into this, heat it in the oven for about 15 minutes, then turn out onto a dish and serve.

SAVOURY VEGETABLE PIE

Different vegetables, such as diced carrot, chopped marrow or beans, may also be used for this pie, which can be covered with shortcrust or puff pastry, and is equally tasty served hot or cold.

8 oz/450 g/$^1/_2$ lb cooked new
   potatoes
4 oz/125 g/$^1/_4$ lb small macaroni or
   vermicelli
4 oz/125 g/$^3/_4$ cup shelled peas
1 lb/450 g/1 lb tomatoes
1 tbsp each chopped onion and
   parsley

3 hard-boiled eggs
$^1/_2$ pt/300 ml/1$^1/_4$ cups white sauce
   (see page 57)
salt and pepper to taste
12 oz/350 g/$^3/_4$ lb shortcrust or puff
   pastry

Cook the macaroni in boiling salted water until tender, and drain. Butter a large pie-dish, put a layer of sliced tomatoes in first, then a layer each of potatoes, peas and macaroni, sprinkling the layers with onion, parsley and seasonings. Continue until the dish is full, put a layer of sliced egg on top and pour the white sauce over this. Roll out the pastry and cover the pie; brush it over with a little beaten egg, then bake in a hot oven (400°F/200°C/Mark 6) for about 1 hour until golden brown.

VEGETABLE DISHES AND SALADS

The Crab-apple trees and bushes are looking very beautiful now, covered with pink blossom and crimson buds.

Wild Pear (*Pyrus Communis*)

VEGETABLE DISHES AND SALADS

Salads, like other vegetable dishes, assumed increasing importance to the cooks and dietitians of Victorian and Edwardian times. Great care was taken to make salads look and taste interesting — here are some of them.

WINTER SALADS

CAULIFLOWER AND BEETROOT SALAD

1 cooked cauliflower
2 large cooked beetroot

1 large tbsp minced parsley or
grated carrot
pepper and salt

Cook the cauliflower till tender but not too soft; peel and slice the beetroot. Divide the cauliflower into florets, season them and pile them in the centre of a dish; pour the preferred dressing over it, and garnish with carrot or parsley. Arrange the beetroot round the edge of the dish. Alternatively, dice the beetroot, and place the cauliflower head down on the dish; cut away the main stalk, then pile the beetroot in the centre of the cauliflower. Pour the dressing over the beetroot so that it overflows down the sides of the cauliflower, and sprinkle with carrot or parsley. Serve at once.

CELERY AND APPLE SALAD

4 sticks celery
2 russet apples
1-2 tbsp chopped endive

6 oz/175 g/1½ cups chopped nuts
light salad dressing

Chop the apples and celery quite small; leave the skins on the apples if you wish. Mix in the endive and the nuts, then toss in a light dressing and serve; a lemon-juice dressing is good with this.

STUFFED VEGETABLE SALADS

Though more complicated to prepare, these are worth the extra time and attention, and make a good first course for a special meal.

TOMATO SALAD

6 large ripe tomatoes
3 tbsp crushed pineapple
1 tbsp minced parsley

1 tsp cayenne pepper
6 curly lettuce leaves
½ tsp brown sugar (optional)

Remove the pulp from each tomato with a spoon, leaving a good case for filling; the tops can be sliced off if you wish to use them as lids after stuffing the tomatoes. Mix together the pineapple, tomato pulp and parsley adding a ½ tsp of brown sugar if you wish. Fill the tomatoes with this mixture, then put each one on a lettuce leaf on individual dishes; pour a spoonful of creamy mayonnaise or salad dressing over each, sprinkle with cayenne pepper and top with a tomato lid. Chill well before serving.

APPLE AND CHEESE SALAD

6 large red apples　　　　　　　　*2 oz/50 g/½ cup chopped walnuts*
2 oz/50 g/½ cup cream cheese　　*¾ tsp ground black pepper*

Cut the tops off the apples, and carefully remove the core and pips. Then scoop out most of the apple and mix the pulp quickly with the lemon juice. Mix together the cheese and walnuts, then stir in the apple, mixing well. Fill the apples with the mixture, sprinkle over a little black pepper and serve at once on lettuce or watercress; if you wish, a little fresh cream or mayonnaise may be spooned over the apples, but with a good cream cheese this is not really needed. Celery and grated cheese mixed make a good alternative stuffing.

LETTUCE AND GRAPEFRUIT SALAD

1 grapefruit, peeled and sliced　　*juice of 1 lemon*
1 apple　　　　　　　　　　　　*beetroot, and yolk of 1 hard-boiled*
1 lettuce　　　　　　　　　　　　*egg to decorate*

Peel and core the apple and slice it finely; sprinkle it with a little lemon juice. Wash and dry the lettuce; reserve some large leaves; shred the rest finely and place in a salad bowl. This part of the lettuce can be tossed in a little light lemon dressing (see page 61) or left plain if you prefer. Arrange the larger leaves on top of the shredded lettuce, and put into each leaf a piece of grapefruit and some apple slices; sprinkle with the remaining lemon juice; place diced beetroot, sprinkled with sieved egg yolk, around the lettuce leaves as decoration.

WATERCRESS SALAD

1 lettuce　　　　　　　　　　　　*1 tsp made mustard*
1 bunch of watercress　　　　　　*juice of 1 lemon*
3 or 4 spring onions (scallions)　　*salt and pepper*
1 tsp thick cream

Wash the lettuce and watercress and drain them well but do not crush the leaves. Chop the onions finely; place the lettuce and watercress in a salad bowl and sprinkle them with the onion. Mix together with the cream, mustard and a little salt and pepper, then gradually add the lemon juice to them. Pour this over the salad, shake the bowl once or twice, and serve at once.

7 PUDDINGS

Thrush feeding
on the berries
of the Rowan
or Mountain Ash.
(Pyrus aucuparia)

PUDDINGS

I brought home a big bunch of Blue-bells, Red Campion, and Wild Beaked-Parsley, the latter is showing it's white umbels of blossom in every hedge-row.

Blackberry

The making of puddings of all kinds had developed into a fine art by Edwardian times. Recipes abounded, from the substantial boiled or baked puddings that helped to fill up hungry families to the chilled delicacies that graced the formal dinner table. Here is a selection, including some familiar, well-loved dishes.

BAKED APPLE DUMPLINGS

6 medium-sized cooking apples
4 oz/125 g/3/4 cup currants or raisins

1 oz/25 g/2 tbsp soft brown sugar
1/4 tsp cinnamon

FOR THE SHORTCRUST PASTRY:

8 oz/225 g/2 cups self-raising flour
2 oz/50 g/1/4 cup margarine or
  butter

2 oz/50 g/1/4 cup cooking fat or lard
water to mix

To make the shortcrust pastry, rub the fats into the flour until the mixture is like fine crumbs; mix to a soft dough with the water, using a knife to mix and lightly kneading with floured hands. Divide the paste into six, shape each piece into a ball, and roll them out thinly to make circles large enough to cover the apples. Peel and core the apples, place each on a circle of pastry and fill the centres of each apple with a mixture of currants, sugar and cinnamon. Moisten the edges of the pastry and cover the apples, pressing the edges well together to seal the pastry. Brush them over with a little milk or water mixed with 1 tsp sugar, put them on a baking-tin and cook them in a moderate oven (350°F/180°C/Mark 4) for about 30 minutes. Serve hot with cream or custard sauce, or try molasses sauce, which is delicious with apple puddings.

GRANDMOTHER'S APPLE PIES

This recipe is made using the same ingredients as apple dumplings; the amount of pastry used in the apple dumpling recipe will make one large or two smaller pies, using round fairly deep plates or tins. Grease these and cover with pastry, then arrange the thinly sliced apples so that they are closely packed. Sprinkle over 1 tbsp cold water or lemon juice, then the currants, sugar and cinnamon. Moisten the edges of the paste and fit a pastry lid over the top, pressing well to seal the edges. Trim, and prick lightly with a fork, then brush over with sugar and milk or water. Bake in a hot oven (400°F/200°C/Mark 6) for about 30 minutes.

Arums, all in flower, — The ground was covered with Wild
out very conspicuously their pale green spathes gleaming
the rabbits burrow. against the red earthen banks where

Blackberry

APPLE FLORY

'Flory' or 'Florentine' tarts have a long history; prunes, plums or damsons used to be served in this way, either as small or large tarts. Puff pastry, for which the recipe is given below, is usually used; it should be cooled before use. For apple flory, line a greased tart or pie plate with puff pastry rolled out to ¼ in (½ cm) thick. Arrange over it a layer of sliced apples sprinkled with ½ tsp ground cinnamon, spread a layer of thick orange marmalade or apricot jam on top of the apples. Cover with a pastry lid, and bake in a very hot oven (450°F/230°C/Mark 8), reducing the heat after 10 minutes to 400°F/200°C/Mark 6. When golden brown remove from the oven; serve either hot or cold, with cream.

PUFF PASTRY:

8 oz/225 g/2 cups plain flour
8 oz/225 g/2 sticks butter

½ tsp strained lemon juice
¼ pt/150 ml/⅓ cup cold water

A good way of making the butter cool and flexible, as it needs to be for this pastry, is to wrap it in a cold wet cloth, and squeeze it to the right consistency. Shape it into a square and put it in a cool place. Sift the flour onto a board, in as cool a place as possible, make a well in the centre and pour in the water and lemon juice; mix to a consistency similar to that of the butter. Knead the paste quickly and lightly then roll it out into a strip twice the length of the butter and about ½ in (1 cm) wider. Place the butter on one side of the paste and fold this over to cover the butter, then seal the edges by pressing with the rolling pin. Cover with a cloth and allow it to 'rest' in a cool place for 15 minutes. Roll it out again to about 3 times its original length, then fold it in three, and turn it so that the folds are to the left and right; repeat this rolling and folding then leave the paste to rest in a cool place for 15 minutes. The pastry is rolled out, folded and turned in this way, with a 15 minute rest, a second and third time — six rollings in all. After the third rest it is ready to use. Make sure that the board is kept lightly floured, and sprinkle the paste with flour from time to time; keep the rolling light and even, with a forward movement, to retain as much air as possible in the paste.

PUDDINGS

I noticed the flower just coming on the Beech, scarcely disting-uishable from the tender green of the foliage. Oak-apples are plentiful now on the Oak-trees.

Blackberry

QUINCE CUSTARD

This can be made with stewed apples or pears but is specially good with the tart flavour of quinces if these are available.

1 lb/450 g/1 lb quinces or apples
2 egg yolks
1 egg white
1/2 pt/300 ml/1 1/4 cups milk

3 oz/75 g/6 tbsp sugar
few drops almond or vanilla essence

Peel core and quarter the quinces; stew them in a little water until they are soft — they will take longer than pears or apples. Crush or sieve them and sweeten with the sugar, reserving a tablespoonful of sugar for the custard; put the fruit in a dish to cool. Heat the milk and beat together the eggs and sugar till thick. Pour in the heated milk, stirring quickly; then place the bowl in a pan of boiling water over low heat and stir until the custard is thick enough to coat the back of the spoon. Remove from heat, and add a few drops of almond or vanilla essence, stir, and allow to cool before pouring over the cooled quinces. When the custard is cold, decorate it with whipped cream and chopped almonds if you wish.

SUMMER PUDDING

A very simple old-fashioned pudding, useful when there is plenty of fruit in the garden. A mixture of fruits may be used — red or blackcurrants, raspberries or strawberries go well together; gooseberries and blackberries are good on their own or with apple.

1 lb/450 g/1 lb fruit
1/2 lb/225 g/1/2 lb sugar
slices of stale bread

Stew the fruit in a small amount of water until it is tender; stir in the sugar until it is dissolved. Line a basin or mould with some of the bread; bring the fruit to boiling point then put it in layers with more of the bread until the basin is full. Finish with a covering of bread; place a plate on top and put a weight on this; leave in a cool place until the next day, then turn out the pudding onto a serving-dish. Pour cream or cold custard sauce over, or, for a change, try it with ice cream.

I also gathered the Yellow Weasel Snout, Lady's Mantle, Field Scorpion Grass and the Garlic, the latter just breaking through it's green sheathe.

Blackberry

FRUIT CREAM

Any kind of fruit purée may be used for this — apricots, raspberries and gooseberries are particularly suitable since they give the cream a good colour; apples, pears or other pale fruits can have a few drops of colouring added if you wish. The cream is made using the following proportions.

1/2 pt/300 ml/1 cup fruit purée   *1/2 lb/225 g/1 cup sugar*
1/2 pt/300 ml/1 cup cream

Some fresh soft fruits, like raspberries, can be sieved to make a purée without cooking; other fruit should be stewed gently in a little water until soft, then sieved to make the purée. Measure, and add the sugar. Stir the cream into the cooled purée and whisk until it is very thick; pour into individual glass dishes and chill for at least 1 hour before serving.

VELVET CREAM

This recipe appears in many old cookery books, both in this simple form and with additions such as coffee, sieved fruit or grated chocolate. It can be used on its own as a light sweet.

1/2 pt/300 ml/1 1/4 cups fresh milk   *1 tsp sherry or 1/4 tsp vanilla essence*
1/2 pt/300 ml/1 1/4 cups cream   *or 1/2 tsp grated lemon or orange*
1/2 oz/15 g/1 tbsp powdered gelatine   *rind*
2 egg yolks   *2 oz/50 g/1/4 cup castor sugar (fine*
                                          sugar)

Dissolve the gelatine in a little water. Beat the egg yolks and sugar together in a bowl, pour in the boiling milk, stir well and return to the pan. Add the gelatine, stir, and cook the mixture until it begins to thicken. Remove from the heat, add the flavouring and cool the mixture a little before putting in the cream; chill and serve in a glass bowl.

For Coffee Cream, add 2-3 tbsp of strong coffee to the milk; for Chocolate Cream, dissolve 2-3 tbsp of grated chocolate in 2-3 tbsp hot water, and add it when the milk boils.

PUDDINGS

The common was covered with short grass and furze bushes and smelt deliciously of Thyme, though we found none quite in flower. There were any number of little flowers growing on the turf, quantities of purple and red Milkwort, Tormentil, Meadow Lousewort.

Blackberry

JUNKET

1 pt/550 ml/2¹/₂ cups fresh milk	2 tsp sugar
2 tsp rennet	1 tsp brandy

Warm the milk but do not boil it. Add the sugar, rennet and brandy and pour the mixture into a bowl or dish. Put it into a cool place to set, then sprinkle over it a little ground nutmeg or cinnamon, or decorate it with whipped cream and some finely chopped nuts. Junket is good with stewed fruit of all kinds.

Puddings made with bread have formed part of English country cooking for a very long time. They are easily made, and good whether eaten hot or cold.

NURSERY PUDDING

4 slices thin bread-and-butter	1 egg
2 oz/50 g/¹/₄ cup granulated sugar	¹/₂ pt/300 ml/1¹/₄ cups milk
2 oz/50 g/¹/₃ cup currants	a little ground nutmeg
2 oz/50 g/¹/₃ cup raisins	

Butter a pie-dish. Mix together the fruit and sugar, and put a layer of these in the bottom of the dish. Place on top two slices of bread, cut into quarters, then add a second layer of fruit; cover this with the remaining quarters of bread, put the rest of the fruit over them and pour in the egg and milk beaten together. Sprinkle over a little nutmeg, then bake the pudding in a fairly slow oven (300°F/150°C/Mark 2) for about 1 hour until set and beginning to brown.

QUEEN OF PUDDINGS

1 pt/100 g/2¹/₂ cups soft breadcrumbs	rind of 1 lemon
1 pt/550 ml/2¹/₂ cups milk	2 eggs
4 oz/125 g/¹/₂ cup castor sugar (fine sugar)	2-3 tbsp raspberry or other jam

Separate the eggs, and put the yolks into a bowl with the breadcrumbs, half the sugar and the lemon rind. Pour in the warmed milk and beat until well mixed. Put the mixture into a buttered pie-dish and bake slowly for about 45 minutes in a cool oven (300°F/150°C/Mark 3) until set. Remove the dish from the oven and spread the jam over the pudding; beat the egg whites to a stiff meringue with the remaining sugar and spread the meringue mixture on top of the jam. Replace the pudding in the oven and bake until the top is a delicate brown.

CANARY PUDDING

A light, simple steamed pudding, this can be flavoured to taste, with orange or lemon peel, or a few drops of vanilla or almond essence.

3 eggs
the weight of 3 eggs in butter and
*   flour*

the weight of 2 eggs in sugar
1 tsp baking powder
1/2 tsp lemon peel

Beat the sugar and butter to a cream, sift in the baking powder and flour. Add the lightly beaten egg yolks, stir well, then fold in the beaten egg whites. Put the mixture in a buttered pudding-basin, cover with a piece of greased paper, then tie with a cloth and steam in boiling water for 2 hours. To serve, turn the pudding out onto a dish; it may be served with a sauce poured over it.

CHRISTMAS PUDDING

The following recipe will make two medium-sized plum puddings; traditionally they should be made some weeks before Christmas, as keeping them enhances the flavour, but they are also good when freshly made.

1/2 lb/225 g/1/2 lb soft brown sugar
1/2 lb/225 g/1/2 lb shredded suet
1/2 lb/225 g/1/2 lb sultanas
1/2 lb/225 g/1/2 lb raisins, stoned and
*   halved*
4 oz/125 g/2/3 cup candied peel,
*   chopped*
2 oz/50 g/1/2 cup sweet almonds,
*   shredded*

1 tbsp minced apple
1/4 tsp ground nutmeg
1/4 tsp ground cinnamon or cloves
1/4 tsp salt
4 eggs
1/4 pt/150 ml/2/3 cup milk
2 tbsp brandy

Mix together all the dry ingredients, adding the apple and spices with the fruit. Beat the eggs well; stir them in, adding the milk and brandy to make a stiff consistency. Place a circle of greased paper at the bottom of each basin; butter the basins well. Put in the mixture, and place a circle of greased paper over each pudding; tie the tops of the basins with well floured pudding-cloths and steam for about 5 hours. Make sure that the water comes about half-way up the basins, and keep it bubbling steadily. To store the puddings, allow them to cool, then put well greased paper over the tops; tie them in a thick layer of paper or clean cloths, or make a lid from foil. They will need about 2 hours steady steaming before use; serve them with brandy butter and cream or custard sauce (see page 61).

8 *AFTERNOON TEA*

Sweet Violet (Viola odorata)

The e were great numbers of birds, chiefly Linnets and Warblers, flitting about among the furze, I also noticed a pair of Whin-chats and some Tit-larks.

Dog Violet (Viola canina)

E dwardian cookery books contain many recipes appropriate for tea-time, whether as a quiet family occasion or a more elaborate social affair. Sometimes a cook's personal collection gives the names of friends and relations who have contributed recipes or household hints. Here is 'Edith's Cake', to which was added a further note from the cook — 'expensive'.

EDITH'S CAKE

8 oz/225 g/2 sticks butter
8 oz/225 g/1 good cup castor sugar
  (fine sugar)
6 eggs

2 oz/50 g/¹/₃ cup sultanas or finely chopped nuts or 1 tsp orange or lemon juice, or ¹/₄ tsp almond essence
8 oz/225 g/2 cups self-raising flour

Beat the butter and sugar to a fine cream together with one egg already beaten separately. Then add the remaining eggs one at a time, beating each in well. Add sultanas or nuts or flavouring, then sift in the flour and mix lightly. Bake in a moderately hot oven (375°F/190°C/Mark 5) for about 30 minutes. The mixture may be divided between two larger or three smaller cake tins, greased and floured, and the baking time will vary accordingly. When cold sandwich together and ice.

For filling and icing:
Boil 1½ cupfuls of granulated sugar in ½ cupful of milk or water for 10 minutes. Stir in sieved icing sugar until thick. Add chopped nuts or orange, lemon or almond flavouring to taste.

SIMNEL CAKE

Often traditional English cake recipes found their way into family cook books. This one for Simnel Cake, always eaten as part of the Easter celebrations, comes from Lancashire, home of several versions of this kind of almond cake. The icing, which is baked with the cake, should be prepared first.

FOR THE ICING:

2 egg whites
6 oz/175 g/1½ cups ground almonds

8 oz/225 g/1³/₄ cups sieved icing sugar
1 large or 2 small tbsp brandy

Mix the almonds and sugar together in a large bowl; make a well in the middle and pour in the egg whites, lightly whisked with a fork, and then the brandy. Stir well to a soft consistency, and keep cool whilst making the cake.

AFTERNOON TEA

I gathered some Figwort and Celery-leaved Crowfoot this afternoon in a ditch in Elmdon Park. Also found the Bittersweet, Black Bryony and Creeping Cinquefoil in flower.

Dog Violet (Viola canina)

FOR THE CAKE:

8 oz/225 g/1 good cup castor sugar
(fine sugar)
8 oz/225 g/1 cup fresh butter
6 eggs
8 oz/225 g/2 cups plain flour

8 oz/225 g/1½ cups candied peel
8 oz/225 g/1½ cups currants
1 large or 2 small tbsp each of
grated lemon peel and juice

Beat butter and sugar to a cream; when quite smooth work in the eggs, one at a time or the mixture will curdle. Beat well, then fold in lightly the sifted flour; add the peel, cleaned currants and lemon juice. Mix well, then pour half the mixture into a tin lined with greased paper. Put a layer of icing over the mixture in the tin, then spoon the rest of the cake mixture over the icing. Lay a thin cover of icing on top, cover the cake with greased paper and bake for about 1 hour in a moderate oven (350°F/180°C/Mark 4).

A SPECIAL CHOCOLATE CAKE

8 oz/225 g/2 cups flour
6 oz/175 g/6 oz good dark chocolate
6 oz/175 g/¾ cup castor sugar (fine
sugar)
4 oz/125 g/⅔ cup sultanas
4 oz/125 g/1 stick butter

3 eggs
1 tsp baking powder
¼ tsp vanilla essence
½ tsp ground cinnamon
1 tbsp milk

Dissolve the chocolate in the milk in a basin over hot water. Cream the butter and sugar together, and beat in the chocolate. Gradually add the well beaten eggs, then the vanilla essence, and sift in the flour, baking-powder and cinnamon; mix well, and stir in the sultanas. Add a little water if the mixture is too stiff (it should just drop from the spoon), then put it into a greased and floured cake tin. Bake for about 45 minutes in a moderately hot oven (375°F/190°C/Mark 5); cool and ice with melted chocolate or a thin glacé icing.

ORANGE VICTORIA SANDWICH

A simple cake for afternoon tea, this made then, as now, a useful stand-by.

4 oz/125 g/1 stick butter
4 oz/125 g/1 cup castor sugar (fine
sugar)
4 eggs and their weight in flour

1 large or 2 small tsp baking powder
grated rind of 1 orange
1 large or 2 small tbsp strained
orange juice

Cream butter and sugar together, beat eggs separately then beat well into the mixture. Sift flour and baking powder together; add them gradually, then lastly add the orange rind and juice. Bake in a

AFTERNOON TEA

Wild Guelder Rose, Elderberry and Wild Angelica in blossom.

Dog Violet (Viola canina)

greased and floured cake tin in a moderately hot oven (375°F/190°C/ Mark 5) for about 30 minutes. Ice when cool.

FOR ICING:

8 oz/225 g/1 cup icing sugar
1/8 pt/75 ml/1/3 cup strained orange juice

Work the sifted sugar into the juice gradually to give the consistency of thick cream; spread on the cake and smooth with a knife dipped in hot water — this should be a fine glaze, rather than a thick icing.

PLUM CAKE

A rich, dark cake, this can be made using double quantities for Christmas or a birthday.

1/2 lb/225 g/2 cups flour
6 oz/175 g/1 1/2 sticks butter or margarine
6 oz/175 g/3/4 cup soft brown sugar
2 oz/50 g/1/2 cup chopped almonds
2 oz/50 g/3 tbsp treacle
4 oz/125 g/2/3 cup chopped candied peel

4 oz/125 g/2/3 cup currants
8 oz/225 g/1 1/4 cups raisins
3 eggs
1/4 tsp bicarbonate of soda (baking soda)
a little milk if necessary

Grease and line a deep cake tin. Cream the sugar and butter; beat in the eggs, one at a time. Sift in the flour and bicarbonate of soda. Warm the treacle a little, and stir it in, then add the fruit, peel and almonds; add milk if needed to give a stiff but not dry consistency. Bake in a very moderate oven (325°F/160°C/Mark 3) for 2 1/2-3 hours; put a piece of brown paper over the top for the last hour of cooking if the cake seems to be browning too quickly.

LANCASHIRE PARKIN

7 oz/200 g/1 3/4 cups flour
4 oz/125 g/1 cup fine oatmeal
3 oz/75 g/3/4 stick butter or 6 tbsp lard
2 oz/50 g/1/4 cup granulated sugar
6 oz/175 g/1/2 cup treacle or golden syrup

1 tsp mixed spice
1/2 tsp bicarbonate of soda (baking soda)
1 tbsp milk

In a large bowl, rub the butter into the flour until it is like fine crumbs; stir in the oatmeal, sugar and spice. Warm the milk and treacle together in a heavy pan, then add the bicarbonate of soda

AFTERNOON TEA

Saw the first Wild Rose in bloom,— a fine pink one, on the top of
a high hedge.; also Blackberry in blossom. The Roses and
Honeysuckle are full of bud, but they are late in bloom this year,
owing to the long spell of cold weather

Dog Violet (Viola canina)

and stir well until this is dissolved. Make a well in the flour mixture, pour in the milk and treacle and mix very thoroughly using a wooden spoon. Grease and flour a large loaf tin, pour in the mixture and bake in a fairly slow oven (300°F/150°C/Mark 2) for 45 minutes or until golden brown. Test with a skewer — if it comes out cleanly the loaf is ready. Cool a little before turning it out of the tin; it is delicious eaten while still hot, but will keep well if necessary.

MELTING MOMENTS

These extra light little cakes can simply be dusted with sieved icing sugar or castor sugar before serving.

8 oz/225 g/2 cups cornflour (cornstarch)
6 oz/175 g/¾ cup margarine or butter
3 oz/75 g/6 tbsp castor sugar (fine sugar)

1 tsp baking powder
2 eggs
a few drops vanilla essence

Cream the butter and sugar; beat the eggs, add the vanilla, then add to the creamed mixture alternately with the cornflour. Stir in the baking powder. Put small spoonfuls of the mixture into greased patty tins, and bake for about 15 minutes in a moderately hot oven (375°F/190°C/Mark 5) until light golden and firm.

CHOCOLATE NUT BUNS

6 oz/175 g/1½ cups flour
1 oz/25 g/2 tbsp cocoa powder
2 oz/50 g/½ cup cornflour (cornstarch)
3 oz/75 g/6 tbsp granulated sugar
1 tsp baking powder

2 oz/50 g/4 tbsp butter or margarine
2 oz/50 g/½ cup chopped walnuts
2 oz/50 g/⅔ cup chopped raisins
1 egg
1-2 tbsp milk

Sift the flour, cornflour and cocoa together, then rub in the butter. Add the sugar and baking powder, then the walnuts and raisins; mix together with the beaten egg, adding enough milk to make a soft consistency. Grease the patty tins and bake the cakes for about 15 minutes at 375°F/190°C/Mark 5.

DEVONSHIRE SCONES

Traditionally these are served split open, with thick cream and strawberry or raspberry jam, but they are also very good hot, with butter and honey.

AFTERNOON TEA

If when you hear the Cuckoo, you begin to run and count the Cuckoo's crys; and continue running until out of ear-shot, you will add as many years to your life as you count calls. — at least so the old women tell you in Devonshire.

Dog Violet (Viola canina)

1 lb/450 g/4 cups flour
4 level tsp baking powder
3 oz/85 g/³/₄ stick butter
1 oz/25 g/2 tbsp castor sugar (fine
   sugar)

pinch salt
1 egg
1-2 tbsp sour cream or another egg
1-2 tbsp milk

Into a large bowl, sift together the flour, baking powder and salt. Rub in the butter and add the castor sugar, then make a well and break in the egg. Add the cream or second egg, together with 1 tablespoon of milk and with a knife mix together to a stiff consistency; add a second spoonful of milk if the mixture seems to be too dry. Turn it onto a well floured board and roll out to about ⅓ in (1 cm) thick. Cut into rounds, place them on a baking sheet and brush with a little milk or beaten egg. Bake in a hot oven (425°F/220°C/Mark 7).

SCOTCH PANCAKES

Sometimes called pancakes, sometimes drop scones, these can be made in a heavy frying pan or on a girdle or hotplate.

8 oz/225 g/2 cups flour
1 level tsp bicarbonate of soda
   (baking soda)
½ level tsp cream of tartar
1 egg

⅓ pt/200 ml/¾ cup milk or
   buttermilk
½ oz/15 g/1 tbsp castor sugar (fine
   sugar)
a pinch of salt

Mix the dry ingredients together and beat thoroughly to a nice batter, then grease pan with a butter paper. Take a dessertspoonful of the mixture and drop into the pan; allow to cook until small bubbles break on the surface, then turn with a palette knife and cook the other side until the pancake is firm and golden brown. Place hot pancakes between clean cloths until cool enough to eat with butter and jam.

CHESTNUT BISCUITS

These rather special biscuits are best cooked on edible rice paper; they should be dry on the outside and soft in the middle.

½ lb/225 g/½ lb chestnuts
4 oz/125 g/½ cup castor sugar (fine
   sugar)

2 oz/50 g/4 tbsp grated chocolate
1 egg white

Boil the chestnuts until they are very soft, then skin and sieve them; add the sugar. Melt the chocolate in a pan over hot water, and when it is smooth add it to the chestnuts and sugar, stirring well. Beat the egg white until it is very stiff, then quickly fold it into the mixture. Place rice paper on the baking tins and put small heaps of the mixture onto the rice paper; fork the mixture lightly so that it forms little peaks, then bake the biscuits in a warm oven (325°F/170°C/Mark 3) until they are firm and dry on the outside. Cool and serve on the rice paper.

CHRISTMAS BISCUITS

This useful recipe can easily be varied. The biscuits may be cooked plain, then iced when cold; or they may be flavoured with a teaspoonful of grated lemon or orange rind or caraway seeds. For Christmas, the following recipe may be used, and the biscuits iced with a thin glaze or dusted with icing sugar before serving.

8 oz/225 g/2 cups self-raising flour　　*1 beaten egg*
5 oz/150 g/1¼ sticks butter　　*a few drops almond essence*
3 oz/75 g/6 tbsp castor sugar (fine　　*candied peel or glacé cherries to*
*　sugar)*　　*　decorate*
½ tsp ground cinnamon

Rub the butter into the flour, then stir in the sugar and cinnamon; add the egg and almond essence and mix to a firm dough. Roll this out on a floured board to about ¼ in (½ cm) thick, cut in rounds with a fluted cutter and place these on baking sheets, lightly greased with lard or oil. Press a small piece of candied peel or cherry into the centre of each biscuit and bake in a moderate oven (350°F/180°C/Mark 4) until golden brown.

9 DRINKS AND PRESERVES

Yellow-Hammers
feeding in stubble

DRINKS AND PRESERVES

Glorious day after a day of heavy rain. On my weekly ride to
Knowle, saw the following flowers in bloom since I passed
through the lanes a week ago, — Field Knautia, Small Seabious,
Nipple-wort, Water Dropwort, Corn Sow Thistle, Creeping Plume Thistle

Sloe
(Prunus communis)

The making of jams, jellies and pickles, wines and cordials, is all part of the country tradition that there is a use for everything. Even damaged or windfallen fruit, as well as the unexpected gluts of hedgerow or garden produce, were harvested and utilized.

There are many interesting old recipes for homemade drinks, some alcoholic, others made with health-giving leaves or flowers. Some, like cowslip wine, we now avoid making owing to a scarcity of the plants, but there are familiar ones, like sloe gin, which continue to be popular at Christmas or other special occasions. Syrups and vinegars are less frequently made now, but are worth trying if you have a surplus of fruit.

A MAY DRINK

This is ideal for a special summer picnic or party.

about 24 blackcurrant leaves　　*2 oz/50 g/2 oz lump sugar*
bunch of woodruff (a small　　*1-2 tbsp lemon juice*
*　handful)*　　*2 bottles hock or other white wine*

The proportions of the ingredients depend very much on personal taste, and amounts of sugar and lemon especially may be varied; as a guide try the quantities given above. Put the leaves, woodruff, pounded sugar and strained juice into a large jug or bowl, pour over the wine. Keep cool for 30 minutes, stirring occasionally, then serve from the bowl.

A SHOOTING DRINK

A winter speciality, prepared in advance when there are plenty of blackcurrants available. Other fruit, such as raspberries or strawberries, can be used in the same way, but with brandy rather than rum.

blackcurrants　　*rum or gin if preferred*
lump sugar

Make sure that the currants are clean and dry, then put them into a large jar or deep bowl in a wide pan of boiling water. Keep the pan on the boil, until the juice of the fruit is extracted. Strain and measure it, allowing ½ lb/225 g/½ lb sugar to 1 pt/550 ml/2½ cups juice. Dissolve the sugar in the juice over low heat, then boil for 5 minutes, skim and cool. When cold, measure the liquid and add an equal quantity of rum; stir well and bottle. Cork tightly.

Cycled through Strathyre and Lochernhead to St. Fillan's.
at the head of Loch Erne. Hay-making going on in all the
valleys, many of which are flooded with the continuous
rains.

Sloe
(Prunus communis)

STRAWBERRY CIDER CUP

1 lb/450 g/1 lb small ripe
  strawberries
2 oz/50 g/2 oz lump sugar

1 orange or lemon
1¹/₂ pt/850 ml/3¹/₂ cups cider

If large strawberries are used crush or chop them; small ones can be left whole, which looks more attractive. Put them in a large jug or bowl, sprinkle the crushed sugar over them, and add the very finely grated rind and the juice of the orange. Allow them to stand in a warm place for at least 1 hour; pour the cider over, add small pieces of ice if you wish or chill for a short while before serving. Different kinds of cider will require different amounts of sugar, and it is worth experimenting to find your preference.

SLOE GIN

Use clean, whole fruit, firm and ripe but not elderly; it should be pricked over (a darning-needle is best for this) and placed in a clean dry wide-necked bottle or jar. Fill this about two-thirds full, then put in 2 or 3 tbsp crushed lump sugar or preserving sugar, so that the bottle is very nearly full. Pour some good quality gin into the bottle, very carefully so that it seeps down into the sugar and fruit. Cork tightly and stand the bottle in a fairly warm place for at least 3 or 4 months — the longer the better. Some people believe in shaking the bottle as often as you see it, others in leaving the gin to look after itself until it is ready. Then it should be filtered through a piece of fine muslin or similar material, as for jelly, pressing lightly to extract all the juice. It will take several filterings to achieve a good clear colour. Bottle the gin and store it, well-sealed, for several months longer before using it.

ELDERFLOWER CHAMPAGNE

1 gal/4¹/₂ l/10 pt cold water
1¹/₂ lb/675 g/1¹/₂ lb sugar
1 lemon

2 tbsp white wine vinegar
6 heads elderflowers

Make sure that the flowers are fully open and are a sweet-smelling variety. Put all the ingredients together in a large plastic bucket or bowl. The lemon juice should be squeezed and added separately from the chopped rind. Cover and steep for at least 24 hours, then strain the liquid and put it into strong sterilised bottles taking care not to overfill them. Seal carefully and keep them in a cool place for a fortnight, when the champagne should be ready to drink.

DRINKS AND PRESERVES

The berries on tree and bush are beginning to make themselves conspicuous, notably the Rowans, Wild Raspberries, (which are very plentiful in the Highlands) and the hips of a species of Wild Rose which has very large crimson fruit.

Sloe
(Prunus communis)

RHUBARB SHERBET

¹/2 pt/300 ml/1¹/4 cups chopped　　　*3 oz/75 g/3 oz lump sugar*
　young rhubarb　　　　　　　　　　*1 small lemon*
2 pt/1¹/4 l/5 cups water

Bring the rhubarb and water to the boil, then simmer for 20 minutes until it is soft. Rub the sugar and lemon rind together to extract the flavour and colour of the lemon, and place the sugar in a large jug. Strain the rhubarb juice into it, then cover and cool well before serving.

Bottling used to be the standard way of keeping surplus fruit, and some vegetables, for use in lean winter days. Glass or stoneware jars, sealed over with wax or clarified fat, were the usual containers, and the bottling liquids — sugar or honey syrups, vinegar or alcohol — ensured that the fruit stayed whole and usable for months or even years. Now, with the widespread use of freezing as a preserving method, the more time-consuming ways are less attractive; but they are worth remembering and trying occasionally for the specially good flavour and colour that can be achieved. Choose containers that have good airtight lids (such as Kilner or similar jars) and make sure that they are well filled so that air is not trapped at the top. For bottling with water or syrups it is best to follow the recommendations in the special books and leaflets available.

FRUIT IN BRANDY

This is an old way of keeping the very best fruit for a special occasion, such as Christmas, when it can be served in glass dishes with cream or ice-cream and small sponge cakes or shortbread biscuits. Follow the first 1 lb/450 g/1 lb fruit and sugar with different fruits as they come into season: strawberries, loganberries, apricots, cherries and plums can be used.

1 lb/450 g/1 lb ripe strawberries　　　*1 bottle good brandy*
1 lb/450 g/1 lb lump or granulated
　sugar

Use a large jar such as a sweet jar or a stoneware pot, with a tight-fitting lid; make sure it is perfectly clean and dry. Small whole strawberries are best but larger ones quartered can be used; place them in the bottom of the jar, cover with the sugar and pour in the brandy. Seal well, with a layer of greaseproof or brown paper tied

DRINKS AND PRESERVES

There were numbers of Starlings
running round about the cattle as they were feeding, follow-
-ing the animals all round the field, they seemed to be
picking up the insects, disturbed by the animals in browsing

Sloe
(Prunus communis)

over the lid. When the next fruit, with the same amount of sugar, is added, stir the contents of the jar first, then put in fruit and sugar as before. Do this with each addition of fruit and sugar — up to 5 lb/2½ kg/5 lb can be preserved to each bottle of brandy.

SPICED VINEGAR

This is useful for pickling beetroot, onions, cabbage or other vegetables. Whole spices are better than ground ones, and herbs can be added too, including bay, dill and tarragon. The following basic recipe can be varied according to preference.

2 pt/1.15 l/5 cups white vinegar
¼ oz/8 g/¼ oz cinnamon stick
¼ oz/8 g/¼ oz whole cloves
10 peppercorns

¼ oz dill seeds
1 bay leaf
2-3 tarragon leaves

Tie the spices and herbs in a muslin bag and bring this slowly to the boil with the vinegar in a covered pan. Remove from heat and pour into a bowl; cover and leave to stand for several hours, then remove the spices and bottle the vinegar; make sure it is tightly corked in sterilized bottles.

PICKLED BEETROOT

Carefully remove the dirt from the beetroot without breaking the skins; cut off the leaves at least 1 in (3 cm) above the beetroot. Place them in cold well salted water and bring to the boil, then simmer gently for about 1 hour or until tender. They are easiest to peel when they are hot, and should be cut into rounds before being put into the jars. When they are cold fill up the jars with plain or spiced vinegar and seal tightly, using non-metallic lids.

PICKLED RED CABBAGE

Cut the main part of the cabbage into thin slices, discarding the outer leaves. Sprinkle the slices with salt and leave to stand for at least 24 hours, turning them frequently so that all the cabbage is well salted. Drain off the liquid and put the cabbage into jars, packing it closely. Bring spiced vinegar to the boil and when it has boiled for several minutes use it to fill up the jars, then cool and seal.

The lake is noted for the number of large Pike it contains. The walls of the little inn-parlour on the edge of the lake are hung round with fine, stuffed specimens in cases,

Sloe
(*Prunus communis*)

PICKLED ONIONS

Peel small pickling onions or shallots and salt them as for cabbage for 24 hours. Then drain them, put them into jars, and cover them with cold spiced vinegar.

Chutneys and mixed pickles are very popular with cold meats of all kinds, and are easily made; spiced vinegar can be used instead of plain, and the type of seasoning depends on whether hot spicy flavours or milder-tasting mixtures are preferred. To be absolutely smooth, chutneys should be sieved, but often a rougher consistency is better liked.

OXFORD CHUTNEY

1½ lb/700 g/1½ lb each of onions,
   apples, tomatoes
½ lb/225 g/½ lb sugar
1 lb/450 g/1 lb sultanas
2 tsp curry powder

1 tsp cayenne pepper
1 tbsp salt
1 pt/600 ml/2½ cups malt vinegar
2 oz/50 g/2 oz currants

Peel and chop up the apples and onions and slice the tomatoes. Put them in a large pan with all the remaining ingredients; stir well over low heat until the sugar is dissolved, then bring to the boil and simmer steadily for about 1½ hours, stirring occasionally. Cool the mixture, then stir it well and put it into pots.

MUSTARD PICKLE

2 lb/1 kg/2 lb mixed vegetables
   (marrow, cauliflower, onions,
   French or runner beans)
2 pt/1¼ l/5 cups malt vinegar
2 oz/50 g/½ cup flour
½ oz/15 g/1 tbsp turmeric
½ oz/15 g/1 tbsp mustard powder

2 oz/50 g/3 tbsp soft brown sugar
12 peppercorns
12 cloves
½ tsp salt
½ tsp ground black pepper
3-4 tbsp salt

Cut the vegetables into small pieces, sprinkle them well with salt and leave them to stand for 24 hours. Drain off the salt liquid; mix the flour with a spoonful or two of the vinegar, then put the remainder to boil. Add the turmeric, mustard, salt and ground pepper to the flour mixture, then pour on the boiling vinegar a little at a time. Mix well, add the cloves and peppercorns, then pour over the vegetables in a large pan. Put the pan on the stove, stir until it

DRINKS AND PRESERVES

Most of the Chesnut trees were green and vigorous, with wonderful, twisted trunks and covered with fruit, as were the Nut trees.

Sloe
(Prunus communis)

boils, then simmer for about 20 minutes, stirring frequently to keep the mixture from burning. When the vegetables begin to soften, remove the pan, and put the pickle into warmed jars; cover the jars when the pickle is cold.

The ability to make good jams and jellies has long been a matter of pride amongst country cooks. But the general rules are very simple, and equipment need not be elaborate either — a special jelly-bag for straining fruit is not always essential, for example. Though using cheesecloth or muslin, or a fine sieve, will result in less clear jellies, the flavour is still delicious. Mixed fruit jams are the solution when particular fruits are available only in small quantities or when you want to be sure of getting a firm set with fruits that are watery or lacking in pectin. Lemon juice is useful for some jams, too. Always make sure that fruit is clean and not over-ripe, and that jars are well washed and sterilized by drying in a warm oven; they should be warm when filled, and it is best not to disturb set jams or jellies until they are quite cold. Preserving sugar (warmed if possible) usually gives the best results, and it should not be added until the fruit is well broken down by slow cooking; once the sugar is dissolved, rapid boiling is needed until setting point is reached. The old-fashioned test using a cold plate is usually a good guide to setting: the surface of the jam should become wrinkled when the plate is tilted.

CRAB-APPLE JELLY AND CHEESE

These can be made either with green or red crab-apples, which give splendid colour and flavour, or with any not-too-sweet orchard apple. It is wisest not to mix varieties, but windfalls can be used. Since apple pulp is very heavy, a double thickness of muslin or cheesecloth is a good idea for straining; it can be rested on a coarse sieve or colander while the fruit is dripping.

Wipe the apples and remove any bad parts; chop them into fairly small pieces, but do not peel or core them. Put them into a large pan with water to cover, bring to the boil and simmer steadily until the fruit is well broken, with skins and pips separating from the pulp. This can be helped along by occasional breaking up of the fruit with a wooden spoon; more water may be needed as sometimes apples can be rather dry. When they are ready place the pulp in the jelly-bag or piece of muslin (several separate ones may be needed) tie it

DRINKS AND PRESERVES

Blackberries are plenti=ful, and there is a rich harvest of berries of all kinds.

Sloe
(Prunus communis)

at the top and allow the fruit to drip over a large bowl, overnight if possible. Measure the juice, adding 1 lb/450 g/1 lb sugar to 1 pt/550 ml/2½ cups of juice. In a preserving pan, warm the sugar and juice together until the sugar dissolves; stir well, then bring to the boil and keep the mixture at a rapid boil until setting point is reached; test after 10 minutes. While the jelly is still hot pour it into small sterilized hot jars, seal quickly and leave until cold.

CRAB-APPLE CHEESE

Sieve the pulp into a bowl — this should be done with a fairly coarse, strong sieve, using a wooden spoon to press the pulp through. Weigh the bowl before sieving, then the weight of the sieved pulp can be calculated; allow ¾ lb/350 g/¾ lb sugar to each 1 lb/450 g/1 lb of pulp. Sprinkle the sugar over the pulp and leave it in a bowl overnight; if time is short they can be mixed and cooked at once but the colour will be less good. Next day add 1 oz/25 g/1 oz of spice (mixed ground cinnamon, cloves and ginger is good) to each 1 lb/450 g/1 lb of fruit, together with the grated rind and juice of 1 lemon. Test the mixture for flavour and add more spice if you wish, and more lemon juice if the fruit is not very acid. Bring the mixture gently to the boil, making sure it does not stick to the pan, then keep it boiling, stirring constantly, until it is very thick. This should take only 10-15 minutes, then the cheese can be put into small pots and sealed as usual. It can be used straight from the pot, or if you wish it may be turned out onto a small dish, when it should keep its shape if a good set has been obtained.

APPLE AND ELDERBERRY JELLY

This is made like crab-apple jelly but with the addition of ¼ lb/125 g/¼ lb stripped, washed elderberries to 1 lb/500 g/1 lb apples. When the apples are broken down, put in the elderberries and cook until they are soft, then proceed as for crab-apple jelly. Sloes can be added to apple jelly, too, but these need the full cooking time; use half the weight of sloes to apples.

ROWAN JELLY

This is served with game, venison and sometimes with mutton. It can be made with half apples, half rowan berries if you wish. The berries are best for jelly when almost ripe rather than too soft.

Walking through the fields today to Elmdon Park, I saw numbers of the little blue blossoms of the Field Speedwell; these, and Mayweed, Pink Campion and a few belated Blackberry blossoms were the only wild flowers I saw.

Sloe
(*Prunus communis*)

Stalk the berries and wash them well, then cover them with water and simmer steadily until the juice flows well and the berries are soft. Strain, preferably through a jelly-bag or a piece of fine muslin or similar cloth, for several hours. Add 1 lb/450 g/1 lb of preserving sugar to each 1 pt/550 ml/2½ cups of juice. Heat gently until the sugar is dissolved, then boil rapidly until the jelly sets when tested; skim before allowing to cool a little, then put it into warmed jars, and cover when cold. If using apples (either ordinary or crab varieties) prepare these as for apple jelly, then combine the apple juice with the rowan berry juice, measure and proceed as above.

DAMSON CHEESE

This is made in a similar way to crab-apple cheese but without making a jelly; it is a good way of using imperfect fruit.

Wash and stalk the damsons, and put them in a large pan with enough water to cover. Bring them to the boil, then simmer steadily until the fruit is very soft and the stones are separated from the flesh of the fruit. Cool, and remove as many of the stones as possible, then mash the fruit well. Sieve it, and allow 1 lb/450 g/1 lb sugar to each 1 lb/450 g/1 lb of pulp. Bring to the boil when the sugar is dissolved then boil rapidly until the cheese sets. Pot and seal as for crab-apple cheese.

WILD STRAWBERRY JAM

Even a small quantity of this is worth making, for its delicate flavour; the same method can be used for garden strawberries, preferably small varieties which are less watery than larger ones.

1 lb/450 g/1 lb freshly picked   *¾ lb/350 g/¾ lb preserving sugar*
  strawberries   *1 tsp lemon juice*

Take half the sugar and sprinkle it over the washed and well drained fruit. Leave in a bowl for several hours or overnight, to enable the juice to flow. Next day put the fruit and remaining sugar into a pan over low heat; stir until the sugar is dissolved, then bring gently to the boil. Add the lemon juice and boil quickly until setting point is reached — this should not be more than about 10-15 minutes; over-boiling will spoil the flavour.

Hips made a great display all along the route, especially on a wild piece of common land we crossed, covered with Gorse and briars. I noticed great numbers of Finches here, feeding on the berries.

Sloe
(*Prunus communis*)

RASPBERRY JAM

A simple and delicious jam which keeps very well, this is made with equal weights of fruit and preserving sugar. Rinse the pan with water, and put in the fruit; stir it over gentle heat until the juice flows then add the sugar. Keep the heat low until the fruit is well mixed with the dissolved sugar, then bring it quickly to the boil. Boil very quickly for 10 minutes, then test for setting. Skim if needed, then put into hot jars.

SCOTCH MARMALADE

2 lb/1 kg/2 lb Seville oranges
7 lb/3 1/2 kg/ 7 lb sugar (approx.)
5 pt/3 l/12 1/2 cups water

Scrub the oranges and slice them very thinly. Remove the pips and put them to soak in 1/2 pt/300 ml/1 1/4 cups of the water. Cover the sliced oranges with the rest of the water and leave them to soak overnight. Strain the pips, add the water from these to the oranges and water in a large pan; bring to the boil and boil steadily for 2 hours. Cool the pulp and weigh it, allowing 1 lb/450 g/1 lb sugar to 1 lb/450 g/1 lb pulp. Dissolve the warmed sugar in the pulp, then bring to the boil and keep the marmalade boiling until setting point is reached; test after about 20 minutes. Put it into hot jars, cool and cover as usual.

LEMON CURD

1/4 lb/125 g/1/4 lb lump sugar   *2 oz/50 g/1/2 stick butter*
1/4 lb/125 g/1/4 lb castor sugar (fine   *3 eggs*
* sugar)*   *2 lemons*

Melt the butter in a double boiler or in a bowl placed over boiling water. Add the sugar and grated lemon rind then add the strained lemon juice; stir well, then mix in the beaten eggs, stirring constantly until the mixture is well blended and thickened. Do not boil, but keep the mixture moving in one direction while it gets hot; when thick, pour it into hot small jars and seal as for jam.

DRINKS AND PRESERVES

I was shown some wonderfully fine specimens of the Parasol Fungus today, pale fawn, flecked and shaded with darker tones of the same colour.

Sloe
(Prunus communis)

MINCEMEAT

The meat which was traditionally used to make mincemeat has long since been replaced by suet, but sometimes even this is thought to be too rich. Here is an old recipe which omits it altogether; if you wish to include it, add ½ lb/225 g/½ lb shredded suet but remember that alcohol is needed if mincemeat is to be kept any length of time — a wine glass of brandy can also be added.

½ lb/225 g/½ lb raisins
½ lb/225 g/½ lb currants
½ lb/225 g/½ lb sultanas
½ lb/225 g/½ lb soft brown or
  demerara sugar

¼ lb/125 g/¼ lb chopped candied
  peel
1½ lb/675 g/1½ lb apples
1 lemon
1 nutmeg

Stone and chop the raisins and mix them with the other dried fruit and the peel. Peel, core and mince or finely chop the apples; mix them with the fruit. Add the grated rind and the juice of the lemon and the finely grated nutmeg; stir very well and leave to stand in the bowl overnight. If using suet mix this in at the same time as the dried fruit; sprinkle the brandy over with the lemon juice. Next day stir well, put it in clean dry jars, and cover with greaseproof paper.

DRIED FRUITS

Plums, apples and rhubarb can all be dried, and soaked overnight for use in winter puddings. Rhubarb should be skinned and cut into short pieces about 1½ in (3-4 cm); apples are peeled and cored, then cut into rings; plums only need to be wiped to remove the bloom from the fruit. Drying can be done on trays or racks in a warm room or cool oven (up to 225°F/110°C/Mark ¼), until the fruit is thoroughly dried out; leave the fruit at ordinary room temperature for up to 24 hours before putting it into boxes or tins for storage.

DRIED MUSHROOMS

Freshly picked mushrooms can be dried in the same way as fruit. Usually they are strung onto a thread when partially dry, and hung in a warm place until ready for storage in jars. Then they can either be kept whole or powdered for use in soups, stews and sauces; they tend to absorb moisture from the atmosphere and to go mouldy, so it is important to ensure that they dry out in a really warm place; they can also be salted and spiced in the same way as onions, for use in ketchup or pickles.

DRIED HERBS

Although herbs dry well, they do not like light, and are best put into an airing cupboard or a slow oven (225°F/110°C/Mark ¼); damp air will cause them to go mouldy or turn an unpleasant colour, and they will not smell as sweet as when they are properly dried. They should be picked when dry, in good weather, and either tied in bunches to hang in a warm, dark corner, or spread on trays, and turned frequently. When they are dry enough to rub easily, they can be either sieved or rubbed off the stalks, and put into small containers. Tins, boxes or dark-coloured glass jars, which do not allow too much light in, are best, and these should be tightly corked. They can be kept separately or in a mixture, as preferred. The following is a good blend of mixed sweet herbs:

1 oz/25 g/1 oz each of parsley and marjoram
½ oz/15 g/½ oz each of thyme (or lemon thyme) savory, basil

¼ oz/8 g/¼ oz of tarragon and crushed bay leaves

When mixed, the herbs can be either put into jars or tied into small muslin bags and kept for use in soups or meat dishes as appropriate. Dried herbs are much more concentrated in flavour than fresh and should be used more sparingly — usually less than half the quantity is enough.

HERB TEAS

When drying herbs for use in teas, or for herb pillows or pot-pourri, it is best to leave them whole rather than to sieve or rub the leaves. Sage, mint, parsley and lemon balm all used to be popular infusions and though fresh leaves have a more delicate flavour a teaspoonful of dried herbs per person can be used instead; make sure, however, that they are not stale or over-dried. The best results are obtained by covering the pot or mug in which the tea is made, and allowing the herbs to infuse for about 5 minutes. Honey or soft brown sugar are good sweeteners to use, and a little lemon juice added to mint tea is an improvement. This is very good chilled as a hot weather drink.